Does Accent Matter?

Professor John Honey was born in England in 1933, and graduated from the universities of Cambridge, Oxford and Newcastle upon Tyne. For six years he was Professor and Head of the School of Education at Leicester Polytechnic, where he was also Dean of the Faculty of Education, Humanities and Social Science and is now a Visiting Professor. In 1985 he embarked upon a new career as a consultant in English linguistics and the teaching of English as a Foreign Language. This has taken him to many countries around the world, and in 1988 he began an assignment as Professor of English in Bophuthatswana.

Does Accent Matter?

The Pygmalion Factor

JOHN HONEY

faber and faber

LONDON · BOSTON

First published in 1989
by Faber and Faber Limited
3 Queen Square London WC1N 3AU
Reprinted in 1989 (twice)

Phototypeset by Input Typesetting Ltd, London
Printed in Great Britain by
Richard Clay Ltd, Bungay, Suffolk

British Library Cataloguing in Publication Data
Honey, John
Does accent matter?: the pygmalion factor
1. English language. Pronunciation
I. Title
421′.52

ISBN 0–571–15459–X
ISBN 0–571–14509–4 Pbk

For my colleagues and students in Leicester,
Singapore and Bophuthatswana.

"The way you speak can affect your whole life."
The Story of English, BBC TV, 1986

"What may come as a surprise to some people is the accuracy with which an individual's speech reflects his position in society."
R. K. S. Macaulay, 1977

Contents

Preface

This book is addressed not to specialists in linguistics but to the man or woman in the street who is interested in the whole business of accents and the way we react to them. I have therefore avoided technical terms wherever possible, and in particular I have not used the International Phonetic Alphabet, by which leading contemporary dictionaries try to show how words are pronounced. Its symbols, like /ʌ/ and /ʃ/ (which stand for the *u* and the *sh* of a word like 'rush'), are clear to linguistics experts and wonderfully convenient to use among those who understand them, but they are not familiar to the majority of British readers. The ways in which I have described different sounds are easier for most people to recognize, though less exact than the specialist terminology. Inevitably, many of my statements, generalizations and opinions are expressed in ways which academics would want to dispute, or at least to qualify.

I have not been able to exclude specialist jargon entirely, however, and a handful of technical terms are explained in the text. Three of these, 'acrolect', 'mesolect' and 'basilect', are already well established in the vocabulary of the discipline known as sociolinguistics, and the two further terms I use, 'hyperlect' and 'paralect', are fairly obvious extensions of these.

A greater difficulty relates to my use of the words 'marked' and 'unmarked' to describe varieties of the standard English accent which, for reasons explained in Chapter One, is called

RP. These are basic terms in linguistics which indicate the characteristics of a pair of items, one of which has certain distinctive features (which make it the 'marked' item) while the other, 'unmarked' one, does not. Attaching a term like this to a specific accent may initially confuse the non-specialist, for whom a 'marked' accent, or, more specifically a 'marked Cockney accent', expresses a *degree of breadth* of accent. Indeed, one of the problems highlighted by this book is the lack of any established scale on which to measure the breadth of an accent: this is one of several areas of language study that cry out for further research and popularization. As it is, everyday language is actually unhelpful in this instance, since the term 'marked RP' in its popular sense of 'very noticeable' RP is very different from its technical meaning, and certain obvious alternatives also have disadvantages. A '*pronounced* Glaswegian accent' sounds odd since all accents have, by definition, to be pronounced. The fact that we need to perceive a given accent not as some kind of solid, all-or-nothing entity which you either have or you don't, but rather as a point on a very broad scale made up of infinite gradations, is important to recognize, even though it complicates the task of trying to identify and describe it.

As this book is designed to be read by some of that vast number of readers for whom English is a foreign language, as well as by British readers, I have in places amplified references to personalities and institutions with which they might not be so readily familiar.

ONE

What is 'an accent'?

"It is impossible for an Englishman to open his mouth without making another Englishman hate or despise him." That was the judgement of the playwright George Bernard Shaw in 1912, and he was referring primarily to differences of accent. Nor did this hold true simply during the early years of the century. Commentators like the writer George Orwell in the 1940s and the sociologist A. H. Halsey in the 1980s have continued to remind us of the persistence of "the snobbery which brands the tongue of every British child", and a writer in the *Observer* newspaper recently referred to the 1950s as a period in which there were still, in Britain, "two cultural nations: those *with accents*, and those even more absurdly styled as *without accents*". Many would claim that this is indeed the case today.

The attitudes towards accent which all these observers claim to have prevailed in this country for the greater part of the twentieth century are the main subject of this book. How, why, and when did they arise? Are they really prevalent today, or have the British become more tolerant about accents? If not, what should we be doing to promote such tolerance and what exactly could we do that would be effective? Do the speakers of other languages, or of varieties of English spoken elsewhere in the world, operate the same forms of prejudice about differences of accent? And what is the outlook for accent diversity? Can we look forward, perhaps, to a period in the near future when all these speech differences – which have, after all, been diminishing in the course of recent centuries – will disappear altogether, along with their attendant prejudices, so that we all end up speaking the English language with exactly the same accent?

Shaw's pronouncement was set down in the preface to his well-known play *Pygmalion* (written in 1912, first performed in Britain in 1916), which was later made into a musical, and then into a hugely successful film, *My Fair Lady*. It tells the story of a language expert, Professor Higgins, who conceives the idea of turning a Cockney flower-seller, Eliza Doolittle, into a duchess within a period of three months by teaching her "how to speak beautifully". His first concern is to alter her *accent*, then to change other features of her dialect. As the play unfolds, there are hints that there are other things about a twenty-year-old Cockney girl that need to be transformed before she can be "passed off as a duchess at an ambassador's garden party".

Accent is Professor Higgins's main concern because he is a specialist in phonetics, which he defines as "the science of speech". In fact, phonetics is, more precisely, the science of speech *sounds*. We need to be clear about the distinction between accent and dialect, whose main components are as follows:

DIALECT	ACCENT
pronunciation	pronunciation
vocabulary	
grammar	
idiom	

There are some other features which may also characterize dialect (see page 183) but these are the most obvious ones, and they constitute the most important differences between the various regional dialects of British English – for example, Cockney English, Geordie English (spoken in the Newcastle-upon-Tyne area), and Glaswegian English – and of course between those dialects and that particular dialect which we call standard English.

What we loosely call 'vocabulary' is the word-stock of a given variety of a language. Its components may vary between different dialects. In *Pygmalion* both Eliza Doolittle and her father Alfred, a Cockney dustman, complain of being *worrited*, meaning 'harassed' in the sense of 'worried' that we use of a dog worrying a bone or a sheep: 'worrited' also exists in many northern dialects but not in standard English. Mrs Thatcher's use of the dialect word *frit* (for frightened, scared, or in modern popular slang, 'chicken') in an angry 1980s House of Commons exchange has become famous. Again, this word survives in a number of English regional dialects (presumably including Lincolnshire where Mrs Thatcher grew up) but not in standard English. In fact, the Lincolnshire dialect is rich in words which do not exist in most other dialects including standard English like *swath* (bacon rind), *threap* (contradict), *kedge* (paunch), *klink* (excellent, super), *gawning* (staring, similar to standard English's 'gawping'). The same is true of other regional dialects, especially those in which words from the region's rustic past are preserved. The West Country dialect, rooted in Devon and Cornwall, preserves hundreds of distinctive words like the all-purpose *coose* ('to coose a coose woman' is to chase a coarse woman), and *dag* which indicates a smaller size of axe.

At an early stage in the transformation of Eliza Doolittle into a society lady, she says, "Them as pinched it done her in." Professor Higgins has to translate, for her genteel listeners, the term 'do [someone] in' as *kill*; *pinch* does not need translating as it is slang for 'steal' in standard English as well as in many non-standard dialects. But the Cockney forms *done* (for standard English's 'did') and *them as pinched* (for 'those who') illustrate the differences in grammar between this dialect and standard English.

The Doolittles' Cockney dialect contains a large number of grammatical forms which differ from those of standard English, and part of Eliza's transformation involves negotiating these differences. These include non-standard forms for plural verbs (ladies *is*), for negatives (won't pick up no ...), for present-tense forms of the verbs *be* and *have* (I ain't, she ain't, you ain't, etc.), and for past tenses (throwed, has broke, you done, I been). Most dialects of British English have a different grammar from standard English, since they are the descendants of the various regional varieties which for centuries coexisted with the one which, as we shall see, emerged, by a series of fortuitous circumstances, as the 'standard' variety in the fifteenth century. A hundred years ago the Devon dialect was described as having the following forms for the present tense of the verb *to be* ('vur tu be'):

SINGULAR	PLURAL
Oi be	We'm
Thee be	Yü'm
Er be (for he, she and it)	They'm

and R. D. Blackmore's famous novel *Lorna Doone* (1869) contains lines like, "Be the king a coomin? Ef er be, do ee waant tu shutt un?" which are intended to reflect the grammar as well as the pronunciation of the Devon dialect.

Whereas grammar deals in general rules for how we put words together, idiom involves the set forms of speech which are not subject to generalized rules but are peculiar to one language (or one dialect) at any one time. Thus, while in many languages, German for example, the leader of a group may announce, "We are six", it just happens that in standard English the idiom is, "There are six of us." In standard English one may say of some activity, "He does it in the morning", but in some British dialects this becomes *on* a morning and in others *of* a morning. Changes of idiom over the course of time are illustrated by Parson Woodforde's diary entry of two hundred years ago: "She was brought to bed of a child." Writing nowadays one would say 'gave birth to a child', or just 'had a baby'.

The single feature common to both accent and dialect is

4

pronunciation. This in turn has two main ingredients, *accent* and *intonation*. Intonation is the 'tune' of a sentence, which in standard English usually differs between a statement and a question. (Listen to the different 'tunes' of "He's going home", and, "Is he going home?") It is often possible to pick out Welsh speakers of English by the 'tune' of their sentences, and this is also true of speakers of Geordie (Newcastle upon Tyne) or Liverpudlians who speak Scouse. Among overseas varieties of English, Australian English allows a different pattern of intonation, just as Swedish is said to have as compared with the other Scandinavian languages.

But the feature which most readily distinguishes the speakers of English, whether they come from different regions of Britain or elsewhere in the English-speaking world, is not so much the 'tune' of their sentences as their generalized accent; that is, they have a vowel system that consistently pronounces certain vowels differently. Thus, most speakers from the North of England pronouce the *u* sound in *cup, dull*, and *hunt* differently from speakers in the South of England, and there is a similar North/South difference involved in the way the vowel in *bath, dance*, and *castle* is pronounced. Certain consonants, too, may be different – for example, *r* or *s*. In words like *cord, farm*, and *world* speakers from the South-East of England do not pronounce the *r* at all, but in many other parts of England (for example, in parts of Lancashire and in the West Country) the *r* is given a pronunciation similar to that of most varieties of American English. In many varieties of Scottish English the *r* is rolled to produce an even more emphatic sound, so that in the mouths of some Scots *world* becomes two syllables.

The consonant *s* is pronounced differently in varieties of British English, and while all of them would produce a soft (unvoiced) *s* in smoke, the *s* becomes voiced (i.e. a *z* sound) in *base* for many Scottish speakers, and among Yorkshire speakers it is not uncommon for this *z* sound to occur in words like *us*. Since Yorkshire speakers also tend to have the northern feature involving the *u* of *cup, dull, hunt*, etc., their pronunciation of the word *us*, sounding like a short *ooz*, is doubly different from that of standard English. The treatment of *s* may also be reversed: among the same Yorkshire speakers the *s* in *because* (pronounced *z* in standard English) is in this particular case softened (unvoiced) into an *s* sound, and since their *au* sound in this word is longer than that of standard English, they say *becawss* rather than standard English's *becoz*.

A speaker with a standard English accent has a total of some twenty vowel sounds and two dozen consonant sounds. Add together a few major vowel differences, such as the ones we have seen in the pronunciation of the *u* of *cup* and the *a* of *bath*; plus a further range of minute nuances affecting a dozen other vowel sounds; throw in a couple of different consonant sounds, such as we saw in *world* and *us*; and possibly a different system for whether or not to pronounce *h* when it comes at the beginning of a word, and you will end up with an enormous set of permutations representing a wide range of possible differences of generalized accent. Each regional accent in Britain is a slightly different mix of sounds used to pronounce in a distinctive way exactly the same words and sentences spoken by users of the dialect we call standard English. If a regional speaker also uses the grammar, vocabulary, and idiom that are distinctive of his region, then we say he is speaking *dialect*. But if he uses the grammar, vocabulary, and idiom of the standard English found in newspapers, books, magazines, and news bulletins, then all we will notice about his speech is his *accent* – and possibly his intonation.

All this is also true of the other accents in which the English language is spoken, varieties which have grown up outside Britain in areas where the language has a long history of being used.

In the diagram the abbreviations above the line indicate five main categories of English as established throughout the world: British English, American English, and the Englishes of the Old

BrE   AmE   E/OD   E/NC   CnE

Dominions, the New Commonwealth, and the Caribbean. Each such category has subdivisions, indicated by the prongs underneath the line, reflecting further degrees of variation, which include accent. British English is divided, as we have seen, into a number of dialects, one of which has come to be called 'standard English'. The accent most obviously associated with the standard English dialect is called *Received Pronunciation* (RP), a term which echoes the rather old-fashioned sense of 'received' as meaning 'generally accepted' as in the terms 'received opinion' and 'received wisdom', especially by those who are qualified to know.

'American English' is a loose description of the varieties of English spoken in North America (including Canada) and it includes the 'General American' accent which is taken as a standard in the same way as British English has RP; other well-known varieties are 'Southern American', 'Black American', and 'Bostonian', all of them sharing more pronunciation features with each other than they share with any variety of British English, including of course RP. American English differs from British English not only in its accent: it is also a slightly different dialect in that its vocabulary, grammar, and idiom show some differences. We all know of examples like *sidewalk, elevator*, and *faucet* for British English's 'pavement', 'lift', and 'tap'. The differences in grammar and idiom between standard American English and standard British English are, in general, so slight as to be not worth taking space over, though grammatical differences between most forms of Black American, on the one hand, and both standard American English and standard British English, on the other, can be very striking.

The 'Old Dominions' embraces those areas (other than Canada) of extensive settlement before 1900 by people from Britain whose descendants speak varieties of English that are close to British English in grammar and vocabulary as well as accent. They are Australia and New Zealand, and South Africa, a minority of whose white population (and an even smaller proportion of whose non-white population) speak English as their mother tongue.

The fourth category is the New Commonwealth, countries which are, or were, members of the Commonwealth by virtue of having been part of the British Empire, but where English is spoken mostly as a second language, which has become well established in the educational system. This includes the countries of the Indian subcontinent (like Pakistan, India and Sri Lanka), certain countries in South-East Asia (Singapore, Malaysia, and Hong Kong), and some East and West African states. These forms of English vary enormously from each other and also show considerable differences from standard English, to a small extent in grammar, vocabulary, and idiom, but substantially in the way they are pronounced. The 'Indian English accent', the 'Nigerian accent', or the 'Singapore accent' owe their distinctive characteristics to the influence of pronunciation features in the mother tongues of the region concerned, and to the way these features have been passed down to new learners in the school system by local teachers.

The fifth category comprises the speakers of a fascinating set of dialects in the Caribbean whose speech forms reflect the experience of their ancestors, brutally transported as slaves from the west coast of Africa to the West Indies and the adjacent mainland regions of North and South America. A form of English very different from standard British English in its grammar, idiom, and pronunciation evolved, possibly under the influence of the original West African languages which it supplanted. It is a separate category from those in the New Commonwealth because it is normally the first, and indeed the only, language of its speakers: it has a long history and has thus had more opportunity to create a life of its own.

One last category of English speakers must be mentioned: the millions of people around the world who are, in varying degrees, able to speak English as a 'foreign' language. The explosion, especially since the 1960s, in the world-wide demand for English to use for numerous functions associated with modernization and social and technological progress, means that mother-tongue speakers of all the different varieties of English that we have briefly surveyed are heavily outnumbered by all those others in the world who want to be able to speak an internationally intelligible variety of English – generally this means British English or American English. I will largely disregard this last category of foreign speakers in this book, except to note that the major factor determining their pronunciation of English, and making it difficult to reproduce a standard British or American accent with any exactness, is the sound pattern of their own mother tongues.

This book is not, however, a descriptive account of the distinguishing features of these five main categories of English and their sub-varieties: there are several good studies of that already (see page 184). Instead, our concern is to understand better the *attitudes* which are provoked by certain accents: how and why people react to them when they encounter them and the judgements about their speakers which they give rise to. The class system and the rigid divisions of British society, so strongly entrenched in Bernard Shaw's day, persisted into the 1930s and were still apparent in the 1950s, despite the egalitarian changes achieved by the reforming Labour government of 1945–51 and the establishment of the welfare state. They still have echoes in contemporary Britain. The founding fathers of the new society established after the Second World War assumed that the reduction of gross social inequalities and the vast improvement in educational opportunities and social mobility would produce a nation in which the old snobberies, including those associated with accent, would rapidly die out.

Yet this does not seem to have happened, and there are many signs that, although class-consciousness may have changed, *accent*-consciousness is still alive and operative in a great many ways. In our serious newspapers political columnists and other journalists regularly pass comment on the accents of public figures, while television critics discuss the accents of actors, programme presenters, and other television personalities. The correspondence columns of both national and local newspapers frequently carry letters from readers commenting on various forms of accent – favourably, or, more often, unfavourably – and when the BBC uses people with marked regional accents to present radio programmes or to read the news, waves of protest are expressed in letters of complaint to the BBC and sacks of hate-mail to the presenters themselves. Ambitious politicians take pains to modify their accents to make them more accept-able. Writers of contemporary novels and memoirs use obser-vations about accent as a crucial part of the description of character: one of our best contemporary thriller writers, Len Deighton, has about a dozen such comments, which are often extremely perceptive, in a single book, and the humorist Clive James has at least as many in the second volume of his autobi-ography. Most of the characters in Anthony Burgess's recent memoirs are introduced with references to their accent.

These are all superficial manifestations of a widespread truth about the continuing significance of accent in British society in the closing decades of the twentieth century. While large numbers of people, especially the young, are unemployed, serious articles appear in respected newspapers by columnists who claim that unattractive accents hinder their speakers' job prospects, and it is not uncommon for job advertisements to mention 'well-spokenness' as a qualification for certain kinds of occupation.

If someone's accent has indeed the potential to arouse this kind of comment and even to influence his chances in life, then one would expect that the nature of the phenomenon of accent and of the prejudices surrounding it would be a matter on which every citizen would have become deeply informed. Yet here is the paradox: the discussion of accent plays no part in the education of our young people. Indeed, as two Scottish researchers have put it, the subject is virtually taboo in our school system. In Bernard Shaw's day, and against a background in which the majority of children did not receive any secondary education at all, the playwright could rightly complain that: "The English have no respect for their language, and will not teach their children to speak it." But it is possible to argue that the elementary school pupils of eighty years ago had a clearer idea of what constituted 'well-spokenness', and may have had more opportunity to practise acquiring it, than pupils in our school system today. One of the reasons for this is that we have stopped making the automatic assumptions about what it is to be 'well spoken', and whether certain accents can be regarded as attractive or unattractive, that were made in Shaw's day. The idea that a standard English accent had some special claim to be a model for pupils to copy has been increasingly questioned in recent decades both by linguistic theorists and by teachers. To understand where that special claim was supposed to have come from, and the relationship between that standard accent (RP) and all the many other varieties of accent in Britain and elsewhere, we need to make a brief excursion into history.

TWO

Where did RP come from?

The Ancient Britons spoke an early form of Welsh. The English language grew out of the speech of the Angles and Saxons and other Germanic peoples who invaded these islands after the Romans had left in the fifth century AD. This Anglo-Saxon (Old English), further influenced by traces of Celtic and by the Latin of the Christian Church, was what was being spoken in England when William the Conqueror and his Norman followers invaded in 1066. Continuing close links with the continent helped to ensure that, for more than two centuries after the Conquest, French, which was the most influential language in Europe, was also the first language of English kings and of a small proportion of their nobility, although English remained the most commonly spoken language in the kingdom and, by the fourteenth century, reigned supreme.

The displacement in 1066 of Old English as the language of government removed an important standardizing influence, with the result that written English diversified into a number of regional dialects, until a transition period of around forty years from 1430 onwards, during which English effectively replaced Latin and French in the administrative records of central government. Meanwhile the evolution of Middle English out of Old English, from around 1100 onwards, was marked by the progressive enrichment of the vocabulary of English by contact with the Norman French, especially in areas such as law and administration, husbandry and housekeeping, and estate management.

Amid the enormous diversity of fifteenth-century English dialects, Caxton, the first English printer, began in 1476 to implement the communications revolution which brought the printed word into every corner of the land. Not surprisingly, the form of English which he used in his printing reflected the linguistic usages of London. These in turn had by then been heavily influenced by the speech forms of 'Midlands' counties such as Bedfordshire, Northamptonshire, and Leicestershire. Because of the enormous authority of the written word, it was the grammar and vocabulary of this variety that came to be regarded as *standard written* English, though its spelling did not submit to complete regularization for several centuries more. Meanwhile, the ordinary people of England went on *speaking* the dialects of their localities, complete with their distinctive verb forms, vocabularies, and ways of pronouncing particular vowels and consonants. Interestingly, a relatively systematic process of sound change (known to specialists as 'The Great Vowel Shift') affected many of the vowels of most varieties of English between the time of Chaucer and that of Shakespeare. As a result, the *a* sound in Shakespeare's *make* moved a lot closer to our present-day pronunciation than it had been to Chaucer's, which was more like *aa*. Shakespeare's pronunciation of *food* was also more like ours, compared with Chaucer's, whose version was closer to present-day RP *ford*. *House* had moved, by Shakespeare's day, from Chaucer's *hoose* to a sound closer to the vowel in present-day *host*. Shakespeare's pronunciation of *light* and *night* was probably very similar to our own, though in the course of his life he would have heard many people giving a slightly throaty sound to the *gh* (as can still be heard, for example, in Scotland) and also giving the *i* in those two words the short sound (as in *bit*, rather than *bite*). In Chaucer's time both this older pronunciation of *light* and *night*, and the vowel giving 'leet' and 'neet', could be heard in London. Both

Chaucer and Shakespeare rhymed *cut* with our present-day (southern) standard English *put*, as indeed is still the case for English Northcountry folk. In Chaucer's England the *k* in words like *knee* and *knight*, and the *g* in words like *gnaw*, were sounded, as they were also for some of Shakespeare's contemporaries. Whereas Chaucer pronounced the *l* in words like *talk*, *half*, and *calm*, by Shakespeare's time this sound was on its way out, at least for many speakers. One sound which was lost altogether in this transition from Middle English to Modern English was the one used to say words like *fyr* (fire) and *bryd* (bride). This required a very distinctive – and nowadays perhaps 'un-English' – rounding and forwarding of the lips, which the French use for *u* and the Germans for *ü*. That is why in English we find it so difficult to produce more than an Anglicized approximation in borrowed words like *début* and *déjà vu*.

Shakespeare's own accent almost certainly changed during his lifetime. He grew up speaking the Stratford-upon-Avon variant of the Warwickshire dialect. At the hands of a pedantic schoolmaster he became familiar with the 'purer' textbook forms of some sounds, which by now were being promoted by certain writers on elegant speech. Once he had made his way to London he would have been influenced by his association with actors and writers – and their patrons – among whom, as we shall see, an educated standard accent had already begun to establish itself.

But how can we possibly know how Shakespeare and his contemporaries pronounced English? A considerable body of evidence has enabled scholars, by a lot of painstaking detective work, to reconstruct with a high degree of probability the way people in London spoke in that period. The written works of Shakespeare and others have been analysed to see how rhymes, puns, unstandardized spellings, and even metre can suggest how certain sounds resembled, or differed from, each other and from modern forms. Even more valuable are the writings of a number of commentators from that time who attempted to describe the exact sounds of English words, sometimes in comparison with

French or Welsh and sometimes in a context where different regional dialects were discussed.

Not only have we got a very good idea of the way English was pronounced in the sixteenth century, especially in London and the regions covered by the major dialect boundaries, we also know that by the first half of that century, and certainly by the time Shakespeare was born, "there was already a clear idea that there was a correct way of pronouncing English, that some forms of speech had already become a criterion of good birth and education, and that it was deliberately fostered and taught."

The particular form of generalized accent which had come to be regarded as the most 'correct' had a regional base: it belonged to the South of England and was not current in the North or West. In particular, it was the speech associated with London and the Home Counties, specifically "of the shires lying about London within 60 miles and not much more", an area which took in the university towns of Cambridge and Oxford.

Significantly, though, none of those who discussed or attempted to describe it claimed that it was the accent of everybody within that region. So far in this book we have treated dialects and accents as though they belong to regions. Another dimension to the way language is used relates to the specific social groups, including social classes, who use different dialects or accents. For this reason, alongside *regional* dialects and accents we recognize the category, which will become very important in our discussion, of *social* dialects and accents. It is crucial to realize that the direct ancestor of British English's present-day standard accent (RP) was not simply a particular regional one; it was also the property of a limited social group within that region. Contemporaries were quite clear that this group consisted of the Court – the highest social classes and the administrators – together with the gentry (and their educated clerks) in the immediate vicinity of London, plus the important category of the most educated, especially the academics of the only two universities which existed in England before the nineteenth century, Cambridge and Oxford.

These specifications should not surprise us, since it is common to find, in societies which are large enough for social differentiation to develop, that prestige is associated with certain groups which thereby become the subject of imitation by others. Among the commonest criteria for the possession of such prestige are political power, economic power, and 'educatedness'. The connections between London and various centres of political power such as the monarch and what we should nowadays call the civil service are obvious, and the constitutional struggles which led to the limitation of royal power and the extension of the authority of parliament did nothing to reduce the significance of the capital city. Moreover, by the late sixteenth century London had assumed a unique importance in the economic life of the kingdom. The city's position as the literary capital, attracting writers and offering special facilities for staging their plays and publishing their work, as well as its possession of a number of superior educational institutions which served the professions, added the third and possibly crucial ingredient to the formula underlying the adoption of the 'educated' accent of London and its environs as the target to which the ambitious would aspire. Possibly crucial, because unless those available to teach others have access to it themselves and acknowledge its prestige, there is no way in which others who want it can obtain it.

Here we have the beginnings of the present-day divide between the accents of South and North, and between RP and the accents associated with all the other regional and social dialects of the British Isles. In the sixteenth and seventeenth centuries the standard accent was far more limited in its distribution and in its availability as a model than it later became. As yet it had little influence in the North, and south of the River Trent (a boundary cited by commentators even in the sixteenth century) it was used by a far smaller proportion of people than is the case today, and, as we shall see, that is a small enough number (see page 53).

It was by no means the case that all members of the courtly or the educated classes spoke with this accent. A commonly cited example is Sir Walter Raleigh, the courtier who charmed Queen Elizabeth I, though this did not save him from being beheaded under James I. Of Raleigh, who was an exact contemporary of Shakespeare, it was said that, "notwithstanding so great mastership in style, and his conversation with the learnedest and politest persons, yet he spake broad Devonshire to his dying day". Even so, we need to note that Raleigh did not *write* in the Devonshire dialect, but used standard English; moreover the very fact that his younger contemporaries, towards the end of his life, thought his broad regional accent worthy of comment suggests that this was a fairly uncommon phenomenon in a man of his education and courtly associations.

It was, more than anything else, the emergence of an educated class that gave impetus to the development and spread of a standard accent. The expression by southerners of prejudices against the rustic accents of northerners is not new: within a couple of generations of the Norman Conquest the monastic historian William of Malmesbury wrote that northern dialects were incomprehensible to a civilized southern ear; Chaucer made fun of northern speech in his 'Reeve's Tale'; and from Chaucer's day onwards it became common to assume that in the midst of the great diversity of English dialects, one form of English was the best, while others were inferior, corrupt, hideous, or laughable. As the written form of the language began to become standardized through printing and under the powerful influence of the King James Bible (1611) and the 1662 Book of Common Prayer, these prejudices attached themselves to differences of accent, and this sort of assumption is reflected in contemporary literature. When Shakespeare wanted to make Edgar in *King Lear* pretend to be a peasant, he made him use words like *zo, zir, vurther* and *vortnight* which would have been familiar to

17

Elizabethan audiences as being southern (and are still identifiable today as south-*western*) forms.

Though by Shakespeare's time the pronunciation of all the English dialects, including the emerging standard accent, was still undergoing change, the connection between that standard and the concept of 'educatedness' was an important stabilizing influence, and the fact that there was an army of schoolmasters to teach it in its 'correct' form had the effect of conserving its character; only grudgingly did they allow change. Compared with the massive changes, especially in vowel sounds, between Chaucer's time and Shakespeare's, the changes over the next two hundred years were relatively slight, even if the sum total of differences between Shakespeare's English and ours seems large. The most noteworthy was the loss, in standard English, of the *r* sound in a whole range of words like *card* and *port*, a loss which spread throughout south-eastern, central, and parts of northern England by 1800, but did not in the same way affect all of the north-west, the south-west, nor, of course, Scotland. (Scottish English was a major dialect rival of the London-based standard. By 1500 it had established itself, at the expense of Gaelic, as the language of most educated Scots, and with each succeeding century thereafter was to move slightly closer to the London-based variety, though more so in grammar and vocabulary than in accent.)

From England alone some 300,000 emigrants left for North America and the West Indies betwen 1630 and 1690, so we are not surprised to find that the majority of the accents of those regions receiving migrants preserve that *r* which, over the next hundred years or so, was to disappear from RP. In America the retention of this *r* was reinforced by the regional backgrounds of many of the waves of later migrants. In England, the two *a* sounds in words like b*a*th and c*a*stle, and in c*a*t and s*a*d, which were still very fluid by 1600, had settled down by 1800 into something like their present-day versions in RP, with northern England sharing with the Americans a shorter *a* than RP's in *bath* and *castle*. The vowel in *cup* changed in RP to its present version, which contrasts with the northern *cup* vowel, but the latter did not pass into American usage, which shares RP's *cup* vowel alongside such variants as the one which rhymes *cup* with RP's *burp*. Increasing literacy and pressures towards 'correctness' led in England to spelling-pronunciations which caused speakers to restore a whole range of sounds which earlier generations had dropped, like the *l* in *fault*, *vault*, and *soldier*; the second *w* in *awkward* and the sole *w* in *Edward*; the *f* in *handkerchief* and *mastiff*; the *c* in *verdict* and *perfect*; the *t* at the end of *pageant*, *respect*, and *strict*; and the *d* in the middle of the word *London* and at the end of *husband*. Over the same period speakers of the standard English accent learned to drop the final *d* which for centuries had been attached when ordinary folk talked of a *scholard* and his *gownd*.

A change, traceable back to the fourteenth century, by which the sound *er* in a whole class of words came to be pronounced *ar* was in standard English largely reversed by around 1800, with the *ar* sound being retained only in a small number of words like *clerk*, *Derby*, *Berkeley* (in which Americans have completed the regularizing process), *sergeant*, and the abbreviation *varsity* (for university). The American pronunciation of *advertisement*, with the stress on the third rather than the second syllable, may have been current in standard British English (and even more probably in educated Scottish English) in the eighteenth century. The suffix *-ile* was in the eighteenth century normally pronounced in standard English in the way Americans now use, rhyming *fertile* with *myrtle* and making *hostile* indistinguishable from *hostel*: standard English changed to the *-tile* form some time after 1800.

Obviously a brief account such as this cannot do justice to the rich pattern of change in the pronunciation of English in the period we are discussing. These examples are simply clues which show some of the ways in which changes took place in the pronunciation of standard English between 1600 and 1800, even though they were nothing like so numerous as those of the two preceding centuries; and which also show that by 1800 the standard accent of British English (RP) had settled down, in its main essentials, into its present twentieth-century form. Thus, if we could transport ourselves backwards in time into an educated household of around 1800 we would, for the most part, find it very easy to understand what was being said, although the pronunciation of many individual words might bewilder or amuse us. A comparable journey into the world of 1600, landing among educated London speakers, would present us with many communication difficulties, though after a few hours we would probably be able to work out, and make allowances for, the pattern of pronunciation differences. With Chaucer's English of two hundred years before that, there would be really serious problems of comprehension which would be compounded by differences of grammar, vocabulary, and idiom, all of which are considerably further from ours than are Shakespeare's.

Though the grammar of standard English was changing in small ways in the seventeenth and eighteenth centuries and its vocabulary was continuing to expand, one aspect of its pronunciation was constant: its educated speakers were aware that there was a standard form of accent that anyone aspiring to high social position ought to copy. As we have seen, that prestige form was identified with London and a certain radius around it. It is impossible to over-emphasize the importance of London as a model for English pronunciation – despite the co-existence there of both a prestige variety and stigmatized lower-class forms – and the influence of London will constantly recur throughout this book. That influence derived not just from the size of London, which between 1500 and 1800 grew in population from around 50,000 to nearly a million, but from its *disproportionate* size, compared to any other town. In 1600 it was seventeen times the size of its nearest rival (Norwich) and housed well over a tenth of the population. By 1750 London had nearly fourteen times the population of its nearest rival (by now Bristol) and by

1801 (when Manchester was nearest) about twelve times. Before 1700 London had become the largest city in Europe. Whereas between 2 and 3 per cent of the total French population lived in Paris in 1650 and also a century later, London's share of the population rose in that period from 7 to 11 per cent. No wonder the Scottish king James VI, who became King James I of England in 1603, should have exclaimed, "Soon, London will be all England!" The city was a magnet for men and women from all parts of the British Isles as well as for recurrent waves of religious refugees: Protestants from the Low Countries and France, and Jews from Spain and Portugal.

There was, of course, outflow as well as inflow, so that it has been estimated that one adult in six, in the century from 1650 onwards, had direct experience of London life. The gentry flocked to the London 'season'; young men and women went there in search of work. The capital's pre-eminence in trade combined with its being the centre of every aspect of life, including law, government administration, finance, and genteel society. England (as opposed to Scotland and Ireland) had no great provincial cities which were regional capitals with their own cultural and political institutions, local forms of taxation and so on, unlike France, especially before the French Revolution, which helps to remind us that around 1789 barely one in eight of the French population could speak standard French fluently. Indeed, throughout the nineteenth century and possibly until as late as 1914, French was not the first language of a majority of France's citizens. By contrast, England (though not all of Britain) was much more of a cultural and linguistic unity, with London setting the fashions and standards and providing both the opportunities and the mechanisms whereby the lower orders, as well as the gentry and more prosperous townsfolk of the provinces, could 'ape their betters'.

By the eighteenth century, then, there was a long-established tendency for the ambition to get on in the world to lure thousands of people every year to London from all parts of the British

Isles. The eighteenth century was also the golden age for 'experts' to produce books in which they pontificated about 'correct' English, especially the rules of grammar and pronunciation. These two facts – population movement and the need to prescribe 'correct' forms of speech – are closely connected. London contained large numbers of people, both natives and incomers, whose ambitions for upward social mobility were going to be compromised unless they could speak acceptably, and before long a great tribe of writers and elocution teachers came into being to meet this new need. Not surprisingly many of these had themselves come to the capital from elsewhere in the kingdom, especially from Ireland and Scotland, and could claim that their own adaptation to educated London speech forms had equipped them to guide others in the necessary changes – though this did not stop genuine Londoners from challenging the "ridiculous absurdity" of the "pretensions of a native of Aberdeen or of Tipperary to teach the natives of London to speak and read". One of them, the Irishman Thomas Sheridan (father of the playwright Richard Sheridan), a prominent lecturer and writer on 'correct' speech, gave elocution lessons to James Boswell after the latter's arrival in London from Scotland, a necessary step in view of the problems of intelligibility which even educated speakers of Scottish English faced in London, quite apart from the prejudices their accent aroused.

Boswell's place in history derives from his friendship with the great Dr Samuel Johnson, whose famous *Dictionary*, first published in 1755, soon established itself as *the* authority on the 'correct' use of words, some of which it labelled 'vulgar', 'barbarous', 'corrupt', or 'improper' according to Johnson's idiosyncratic prejudices. Johnson had strong views about the Scots, the Irish, and about most foreign countries, and was prepared to snub a lady who questioned him in a broad Scottish accent. Yet when he himself had first arrived in London from his native Lichfield, his upper-class and actor friends were amused at the marked Staffordshire accent he had brought with him, in which *punch* sounded like 'poonsh', *once* 'woonce', and *there* 'theer'. It is probable that his accent became modified to some extent by his long residence in the capital and by his accommodation to the accent of the educated or upper-class Londoners among whom he spent part of his time.

One of these was Mrs Elizabeth Montagu, a formidable society lady at whose literary salon Dr Johnson was a guest for a time. Mrs Montagu had pronounced views on provincial accents and their unacceptability in genteel society "in this polished age", especially in the mouths of young ladies. "The Kentish dialect", she claimed, "is abominable, though not so bad as the Northumberland and some others." There is plenty of evidence that Mrs Montagu's prejudices were not untypical. We might expect such views about accent to flourish in London, but it is significant that by the eighteenth century they were coming to be shared by the upper classes – and their socially ambitious imitators – all over England. Gentry families in the northern counties such as Yorkshire and County Durham were beginning to look to boarding schools in London or the Home Counties, specifically in order to 'correct' their children's accents. The parent of a boy at a *day* school in Birmingham was warned by the headmaster of the danger of his acquiring a "vicious pronunciation" and a "vulgar dialect" outside school hours. Even in a school in London's Kensington in the 1760s, to which a Scottish judge sent his sons so that they might "have the English accent perfectly", this objective could be imperilled by the wrong balance of accents among their schoolfellows, in this case resulting from an "inundation of Scots boys, of which some pour in fresh from the Caledonian mountains . . . to destroy all the arts and civility of the South".

Mrs Montagu shared the view of many of the provincial gentlefolk that the best safeguard against a child's carrying a provincial accent into adult life was a boarding-school education. What girls *learn* at such schools, she claimed, was trifling: more important was what they *unlearned* – "a provincial accent, which is extremely ungenteel" – and improvement in a girl's speech could, she asserted, be expected after as little as one year as a boarder. Unfortunately for the increasing numbers of parents who looked to this remedy, the quality of girls' boarding schools was notoriously unreliable, and boys' schools, even the most prestigious, were, in some respects, even worse. The small number of boys' 'public' (i.e. prestigious private) schools were in this period – and, indeed, up until the middle of the nineteenth century – in a state of constant disciplinary crisis, and they only educated a small proportion of the sons of the upper classes.

Moreover, those boys who braved the disorders, the bullying, the ineffective teaching, and the general corruption of Eton, Harrow, Winchester, Rugby, and a few other similar schools at this time discovered that there was no firm expectation of a standard accent among boys or masters. Some went on speaking with marked traces of local accents all their lives, despite their public school education and possible later attendance at Cambridge or Oxford. This was true of men of great power and national prestige whose privileged education took place before 1870, even when such men lived out their public careers in London. Sir Robert Walpole, the first British Prime Minister, attended Eton and Cambridge, but all his life sounded like a Norfolk squire. The fifteenth Earl of Derby, educated at Rugby and Cambridge, was Foreign Secretary in the 1860s and 1870s, and died in 1893. Disraeli described his lordship's accent as a "Lancashire patois". Even Gladstone, who in 1821 at the age of twelve was "the prettiest little boy who ever went to Eton", and who later studied at Oxford, retained in his accent the traces of a boyhood in Liverpool when a Lancashire accent was commonly heard, before the great influx of the Irish which, mixed with Welsh, helped to produce modern Scouse. Sir Robert Peel grew up in Staffordshire and was at Harrow around 1800, then at Oxford. To the end of his life (1850) he reversed the vowel sounds of RP's *put* ("putt") and the first syllable of *wonderful* "woonderful") and had trouble with his *h*s.

What was crucially lacking to the increasingly accent-conscious parents of the century from the 1760s onwards was a widespread system of boarding education which would guarantee that their children – or at least their sons – would be protected from the already unfashionable local speech forms and would be given access to the standard accent. Boarding education did, of course, exist: in the small number of public schools and in many hundreds of endowed grammar schools and private schools. Their attractiveness to parents increased in the nineteenth century, so that by the 1860s a third of the boys in nearly 800 endowed schools were boarders, and in many localities there was a similar proportion of boarders in private schools. But pupils tended to board within a short distance of their homes, and for a relatively short school life – perhaps only a year or two, which offered no certainty that they would acquire the right accent, despite Mrs Montagu's optimism, and despite frequent references by the schools' heads, and in their prospectuses, to the desirability of pupils' learning to "speak properly". In any case there was as yet no guarantee of the acceptability of the teachers' own accents. After the great parliamentary Reform Bill of 1832 there was a greater concern, at local community level, with class distinctions, and by the 1860s it could be observed that gentry parents preferred "a more distant place of education" for their sons: "It is the object of the father, as a rule, to withdraw his son from local associations, and to take him as far as possible from the sons of his neighbours and dependants." This was especially true of parents in regions like Yorkshire where the differences between the standard accent and local forms were very marked.

It is to Dr Thomas Arnold, headmaster of Rugby School (1828–42), and to his disciples, that credit must be given for the revolution that transformed the public schools into a new type of system which would meet these new demands. What emerged by around 1870 from these changes was a group of fifty or more schools, most of them entirely or substantially boarding schools, whose viability in terms of 'law and order' was secure despite total numbers of around 600 boys or more. Along with improved discipline, they became considerably more effective in both their teaching and, to an even greater degree, in the hold they had on their pupils' attitudes and values. Closer teacher–pupil relations increased the effectiveness of teachers as models for pupils' behaviour and accent. Public schools became more homogeneous; both in respect of their social class intake – in many cases schools found ways of suppressing the rights of the local poor boys to attend – and of age. An infrastructure of preparatory schools grew up, especially from the 1860s onwards, which gave a miniature public school experience to boys aged seven or eight and upwards until they passed into their public schools at thirteen or fourteen. (Winston Churchill, born in 1874, was sent away to prep school when he was seven.)

The two most important facts about the new public school system from around 1870 onwards were the extent to which it was used and the credentials which it supplied. The whole of the upper and upper-middle classes now wanted this kind of education for their sons, and it became the expectation of this sector of society that boys would be sent away from home, first to prep school and then to public school, from the age of seven or eight to seventeen or eighteen – ten highly formative years of their lives. Those who had not undergone this experience had this lack borne in upon them if they went to Cambridge or Oxford, and were later at a similar disadvantage in applying for jobs and commissions in the army as well as in terms of general social acceptability. The ability to answer satisfactorily the question which became all-important after 1870, "Where did you go to school?" became the membership card of the new caste of 'public school men' whose emergence constituted a major development in British social history which is understated and even disregarded in many modern textbooks about this period. A parallel, but not entirely comparable, development in boarding schools for girls took place, though boarding never became as general for girls as it did for boys. The popularity of the model of the school provided by the boys' public schools meant that many institutions of school life which developed among boys – such as prefects, the 'house' system, and compulsory organized games – were simply incorporated wholesale into girls' schools. Because of the amazing popularity of a newly invented literary genre, the school story – read by millions of pupils who themselves had no access to real-life experience of a public school – similar institutions, expectations, and some of the language of public school life, were imported into many other different types of school.

It was the public school system in this new sense which made possible the extension of RP throughout the top layers of British society, and indeed to many people below the top. There is little evidence that, in boys' public schools at least, it was systematically taught. New boys with local accents were simply shamed out of them by the pressure of the school's 'public opinion'. The prep schools, having pupils at an earlier, more formative age, were very important in this respect. In the decades immediately following 1870 there was a time-lag before non-standard accents died out among masters (and indeed headmasters) in the leading public schools. New appointees could be, and were, screened for accent. The boys' reaction to that minority with 'suspect' accents who got through this screening depended upon their general effectiveness as teachers: a weak disciplinarian would find that his accent became another stick with which they would beat or bait him. In a popular man, respected for his teaching or sporting gifts, mildly non-standard speech forms were tolerated – even humoured – as part of the idiosyncrasies of a 'character'.

Given that membership of the new caste of public school men

became so critical after 1870 to an individual's chances in life, it is amazing that there was such imprecision about which schools actually counted as public schools, in any sense which other public school men would have acknowledged when considering an individual for a job, for membership of a club, or even as a potential son-in-law. In fact the network of public schools was delimited, more than anything else, by the ways in which the schools interacted at games, cadet corp camps, and other characteristic activities such as competitive rifle shooting. But how were an individual's claims to be a 'public school man' effectively verified? Public schools invented distinctive ties for their Old Boys to wear, developed Old Boy Associations and published registers of members' names, but for many purposes these only worked when checking out the products of the better known schools. The most easily manageable, if superficial, index of public school status was accent. By the end of the nineteenth century a non-standard accent in a young Englishman signalled non-attendance at a public school, whereas if he spoke RP he was either a genuine member of the new caste of public school men or he had gone to some trouble to adjust his accent elsewhere, thus advertising the fact that he identified with that caste and its values.

And by the end of the nineteenth century there were other ways of acquiring RP than through attendance at preparatory and public schools. As we have seen, Cambridge and Oxford had, since the sixteenth century (or even earlier), tended to foster the standard accent of the educated, though many of their most famous dons, even in the nineteenth century, spoke with marked traces of the regions from which they originated. By the 1880s there were strong pressures on undergraduates at both universities – varying in intensity from college to college – to speak RP. F. E. Smith, who (as Lord Birkenhead) became Lord Chancellor in 1919, went up to Wadham College, Oxford, in 1890 from a day school in Birkenhead with a marked local accent: he is said to have adapted to RP "in about six weeks" at Oxford.

Headmasters and assistant masters at endowed grammar schools and at private schools after 1870 were increasingly influenced by RP, and in the 1880s and 1890s explicit pressures towards RP began to extend down into elementary schools and teacher-training colleges, often at the instigation of government inspectors of schools. The teaching of reading, recitation and dictation in elementary schools became an important vehicle of such pressure: the central government's Education Department prescribed in 1898 the correct method of teaching vowel sounds, and teacher-training colleges offered instruction in elocution. There are few signs that pupils resented this implied assault on their native speech. In areas where there was strong pride in the local dialect, such as parts of the North of England, some individual schools tried to foster local speech forms, with the firm support in at least one area of the government inspector of schools for the locality. But the response of some of the parents is very revealing. They wanted dialect forms kept out of the schools, on the grounds that they preferred that their children "should talk smart when they're grown up". Meanwhile, inspectors and teachers of English in London elementary schools who met in conference in 1906, declared that "The Cockney mode of speech, with its unpleasant twang, is a modern corruption without legitimate credentials, and is unworthy of being the speech of any person in the capital city of the Empire."

So the standardization of English accents in the direction of RP, and at the expense of traditional regional and social-class forms, was partly a result of changes in the educational system. Other social changes also played their part. The growth in the use of the new public school system was, from the 1840s onward, made possible by the new railways. The creation in 1870 of a state-organized system of mass elementary education gave a further incentive to the established middle classes to send their children away to board rather than attend local schools where they would have to mix with the children of their own servants,

with all the consequences for their accents which that implied.*
Railways also threatened the regional dialects, for they speeded
up and intensified a process which had long been under way
– the internal movement of England's (and indeed Britain's)
population from village to village, from village to town, and
from all parts to London. Considerable mobility had been going
on for centuries, but most of it was local, over short distances.
The new scale and pace of mobility, and the industrial and urban
growth† associated with it, had effects on local speech forms
which were already being commented upon by qualified
observers in the 1870s.

But it was the public schools, the preparatory schools, and the
ancient universities which continued to be the main guardians
of RP: public school attendance – or, failing that, an RP accent
– was one of the foremost criteria for being an officer in the
First World War. In Birmingham in 1918 it was possible to buy a
manual designed to enable local speakers to correct their accents,
since, as its author claimed, "to no one is the absence of local
dialect more important than to the young officer in the army".
Carnage at the front forced that specification to be relaxed in
many cases, and men had to be commissioned whose voices
betrayed their promotion from the ranks. When one such officer

* The risk of 'contamination' of children's accents by mixing with servants
remained a preoccupation of middle-class households until the virtual disap-
pearance of traditional forms of domestic service in Britain after 1945.
Ronald Fraser's autobiography *In Search of a Past* recalls how as a boy of
four or five in a Berkshire village in the 1930s he was brusquely reprimanded
by his father for speaking like the gardener; a similar concern caused
"village" children to be kept out of the house. On the other hand, service
in such a household had its compensations for some members of the working
class: as one of them afterwards put it, "You were superior to factory people.
You learned to speak different because you were with people who spoke
well."

† Such growth was exceptional in western Europe, leading to the drastic
reduction of the peasantry. By 1900 England had a rural population which
represented a bare 10 per cent of the total, a tiny proportion compared with
other European countries, including even industrialized Germany.

inspected the cadets at a public school (Lancing) in 1919, the sixteen-year-old Evelyn Waugh helped to organize the dropping of rifles as a demonstration against the man's accent. The requirement of RP was widely believed still to be true for English officers in the Second World War: the public-school-educated actor Dirk Bogarde (born in 1921) claims that in that war the sole reason for his promotion from the ranks to officer status was his accent.

Early this century the linguistic experts began by labelling what they were later to call RP as "PSP" – Public School Pronunciation – and we can see why they did so. The urge of the ambitious to ape their betters led to the introduction in 1916 in a Midlands grammar school – soon to be promoted to the Headmasters' Conference, the mark of public school status – of a scheme designed to improve the boys' accents by chanting, for the first period each morning, a different vowel sound each week; similarly, in girls' grammar schools in this period there was often an emphasis on elocution. But by the 1920s the responsibility of the educational system in general, and of the public schools in particular, for the maintenance and spread of RP was beginning to pass to the new media of mass communication: radio (and later television) broadcasting (the BBC was founded in 1922). This task was reflected in the careful selection of announcers and presenters with RP accents, and in the establishment of the BBC's Advisory Committee on Spoken English (1926), chaired first by the Poet Laureate, Old Etonian Robert Bridges, and then by George Bernard Shaw. Some of the pronunciations of specific words which this committee recommended have a very dated ring today, reminding us of how even 'correct' speech forms change in the course of time. *Profile* was to be pronounced proFEEL; *suave* should rhyme with 'wave'; the stress in *decade* should be on the first syllable and in *balcony* on the second (as indeed balCOny was usually pronounced throughout the nineteenth century): and *vitamin* should be pronounced in the American way, the first syllable rhyming with *bite*. One of

Bridges's main concerns had been for the general restoration of full vowel sounds in unstressed syllables. For more than a century standard English had (for example) turned the first syllable in *congratulate* or *confederate* from *con* to *c'n*. Likewise the second (unstressed) syllable in *parody* or *parasite* is given a kind of *uh* sound rather than that suggested by ROD or RAS. To have implemented such a change would have been equivalent to Canute's attempt to turn back the waves, and it would certainly have made announcers sound pedantic and over-precise, though some Shakespearean actors still feel obliged to attempt it.

If the authorities at the BBC had any doubts about their policy of 'maintaining standards' by insisting on RP speakers – usually public school and Oxbridge men – whose sense of linguistic propriety was enhanced by having to be properly dinner-jacketed while they read the radio news bulletins to their unseeing audiences, then these doubts were soon removed. During the war, the decision was made for security purposes to use a radio personality with a well-known voice and accent to read news bulletins, albeit in a very moderate version of his normal Yorkshire accent. This use of Wilfred Pickles met with a storm of protest from listeners, many claiming that such an accent compromised the credibility of the news bulletin he read. BBC television, which started up briefly just before the Second World War, first reached a mass audience in the early 1950s, and this was immediately followed by the coming of commercial television in 1955, which soon meant that hardly a home in Britain was untouched by the new medium.

It was not until the 1960s that the BBC relaxed its policy of limiting the representation of non-standard accents to the statutory weather forecaster, gardeners' programme panellist, and comedian, to 'countrymen', servants, and policemen in plays and serials, and to victims of inner city decay in searing documentary dramas about social deprivation. However, as we shall see in a later section, there is still a widespread public expectation that certain aspects, at least, of radio and television broadcasting should be transmitted in a standard accent. We also know that from the 1920s to at least the 1960s many people from non-standard accent backgrounds were influenced in the direction of RP by the model presented by BBC radio. The public schools signalled their acknowledgement of the transfer of the guardian-ship of RP to the new broadcasting media during the 1960s when many public schoolboys, in an effort to identify with their peer group in the less privileged (but more exciting) world outside, struggled to shake free of RP and to take on exotic accents like the Liverpool 'Scouse' of the Beatles generation – all this to the dismay of their parents and (because they had in many cases paid the school fees) of their grandparents. Sir Harold Acton (born in 1904), distinguished author, critic, Old Etonian, and 'aesthete', told an interviewer in 1982 how he had revisited his old school "not long ago" to attend a play: "They were all talking Cockney. They acted with enthusiasm, but their accents defeated me."

Though this fashion soon abated, and most public schools resumed the use of informal mechanisms for shaming new boys into dropping the most disparaged accents, this phenomenon does represent a significant departure from the otherwise true generalization that for around eighty years after 1870 anybody with this privileged kind of education was likely to speak with an RP accent. If we examine the composition of the national elite of the period – judges, senior civil servants, diplomats, professors, top headmasters, Cabinet ministers, Anglican bishops, generals, admirals, and so on – we will find several who had not been educated at public schools, but very few indeed who had not adjusted their non-standard accents, especially if they grew up speaking one of the least popular ones, in the direction of RP.

The Church of England was one of the foremost guardians of RP. Earlier this century, elocution courses were offered in at least some Anglican theological colleges, even if those training at the most prestigious ones would never have been admitted without evidence of RP, though traces of educated Scottish or Irish accents were permissible. Of a prominent Anglican clergyman who as a day boy had attended the highly regarded Manchester Grammar School before 1877, his headmaster later commented that he "would have been a bishop if he could have learned to pronounce *sugar* otherwise than to rhyme with *lugger*". In 1917 an educational journal mentioned 'Public School and University English' as a particular characteristic of Anglican clergymen who were graduates of Oxford and Cambridge. In fact, it was not until 1959 that an English suffragan bishop with a noticeable non-standard accent was appointed.

So a non-standard accent in a minister of religion would, until comparatively recently, be a fairly safe indicator that he belonged to a Nonconformist denomination. The accents of Roman Catholic priests and bishops in England have often revealed their Irish or continental origin. But among any of these men of God, a very marked non-standard English accent (other than a foreign accent) would compromise its speaker's claim to 'educatedness' – and this has been true for well over a century. When a former apprentice from Saddleworth, near Oldham in industrial Lancashire, went to study for the Congregationalist ministry in London in 1795, and then to serve as a minister in south-east Essex, he faced the challenge of adapting to an accent which was more acceptable and more intelligible. "Perhaps", he later wrote, "there is no part of England where the provincial accent is so bad as in Saddleworth, and, as I had lived entirely among the lower class my pronunciation was miserably uncouth and repulsive."

The socialist writer Beatrice Webb (daughter of a wealthy and cultivated Victorian businessman) who married Sidney Webb (later, as Lord Passfield, a Labour peer) described in her diary in February 1890 her first meeting with Sidney, then a junior civil servant in the Colonial Office. After outlining his general appearance and character, she came to his most significant feature: "To keep to essentials, his pronunciation is Cockney, his H's are shaky, his attitudes by no means eloquent . . ." Her family and educated middle-class friends reacted as much against his accent and humble background as against his socialist opinions, and she had to brave much opposition, and the desertion of some of her educated friends, when she accepted Sidney's proposal of marriage.

C. H. Rolph, born in 1901, and himself from a modest educational background, became a London police inspector and was later for many years a writer on the socialist *New Statesman*. In his recent memoirs he describes how, as a seventeen-year-old clerk in a clothing firm in the City, he spent months admiring from a distance a strikingly pretty girl who in the course of her work called at his firm each week. But when he eventually plucked up courage to initiate a conversation, his romantic excitement evaporated with the shock of hearing her accent – "the period voice of the East End cockney, ugly and abrasive . . . Having heard her speak, and registered my secret rage that she should have been saddled for life with this ugliest of all versions of my native tongue, I immediately lost interest in her as a girl, and now recall her merely as a method of producing unpleasant noises."

Thus the assumptions about non-standard accents and their social acceptability reflected in Shaw's *Pygmalion* were widely shared, at least in that period. Attempts to cite exceptions to these generalizations about accent prejudice mostly turn out to be misleading. The first soldier to rise from the rank of private to become a field marshal was Sir William Robertson, who was Chief of the Imperial General Staff in the crucial war years of 1915–18. A man of lowly birth in Lincolnshire, he is often described as having "talked with a Cockney accent" and as having dropped his aitches for most of his life. In fact, Robertson was an accomplished linguist who had considerable facility in adapting his accent to suit the occasion. (We also note that he made enormous financial sacrifices as a young officer to send his own son to public school.)

Whereas the school-leaving age for the mass of the population in 1880 was effectively ten, this had slowly risen to fourteen by 1918 and became sixteen in 1972. It became more common for students from working-class homes to enter university in the inter-war years, and after 1945 state payment of fees, and the availability of grants to cover up to 100 per cent of living expenses, put education at a university (and from 1969 at a polytechnic) within the reach of everyone. This exposure of more and more people from all classes to higher and higher levels of education made ever larger numbers aware of the connection between educatedness and the RP accent. Moreover, people's mobility generally had been greatly increased through advances in the speed and ease of travel, by the geographical distribution of work opportunities, and the institution of annual holidays away from home. All these factors have exposed a far greater proportion of the population than hitherto to a variety of accents, often making them conscious of adverse reactions to non-standard ones outside particular regions and social groups. Conscription in two world wars and national (military) service for men between 1947 and 1963 offered a similar opportunity. As a national service corporal afterwards described it: "To be surrounded by so many different accents – Geordie, Scouse, Mancunian, Brummie, Jock, Cockney – was an ear-opener." The evacuation to the countryside of many thousands of schoolchildren from cities like London in the Second World War was another solvent.

It might be thought that the reverse would also have been true and that these factors would together produce a greater tolerance of non-standard accents. The reasons why this did not happen are explored in Chapter Four. None the less in the period since the 1850s there has been a great levelling of dialect and accent differences in Britain. People who are still regarded as speaking a local dialect are far closer to standard English than their grandfathers and great-grandfathers were, even though they are still clearly identifiable as not speaking standard English, as is also true of speakers with non-standard accents. We notice, too, that the continuing prejudices against non-standard accents operate more forcefully against certain accents than against others. We are beginning to see the outlines of a hierarchy of accent prejudice which we must explore after we have first dealt with an important prior distinction – that between the different types of the standard accent itself.

THREE

Talking proper and talking posh

'Received Pronunciation' (RP), the 'Queen's English', 'Oxford English', 'BBC accent', 'public school accent' – all these everyday terms are used to denote the standard accent whose evolution was traced in Chapter Two. Some of them (Queen's English – or depending on the sex of the reigning monarch, King's English – and Oxford English) refer not just to accent but to the standard dialect as a whole. Because it *is* the standard accent and has a high prestige, more effort goes into comparing it with non-standard accents than in analysing the characteristics of RP itself. As soon as we begin to do this, we realize that there is more than one form of RP.

The distinction which I particularly want to draw is between what I have called *marked* and *unmarked* RP. Both are non-regional forms and though a present-day speaker of either may well have come from the South of England, he or she could in fact have originated from anywhere in Britain. *Unmarked RP* suggests a fairly high degree of educatedness, although the social class of its speaker need not be very exalted: he or she may be a primary school teacher, a secretary, a doctor or solicitor, or the archetypal BBC announcer. The *marked RP* speaker definitely sounds as though he or she has had a privileged kind of education, at a leading public school for example, although not necessarily to a very high level. One is tempted to say that the marked RP accent is associated not so much with an 'educated' voice as with a 'cultured' voice. As to social standing, every syllable of the marked RP accent seems to assert a claim to a special degree of social privilege.

While reading the above paragraph, anyone who has been brought up in Britain or who has lived in the country for a long time will already have begun to think of examples of the ways in which marked RP is spoken which distinguish it from unmarked RP, and of individuals and groups of people with whom it is associated: some members of the royal family; dons at Oxford and Cambridge – perhaps not in reality, but certainly in the university atmosphere portrayed in television dramas of the *Brideshead Revisited* kind; senior officers in the armed forces, particularly retired admirals and brigadiers; dukes (and their families) who actually live on and run their vast estates. In the circle of debutantes who used to be presented at court in the year of their 'coming out' marked RP was commonplace, and since the ending of this social ritual in recent years, we have only to look at the Sloane Rangers for sounds which assure us that this special form of RP is alive and well and being passed on to a new generation of the socially privileged and those who try to identify with them.

What are some of its distinctive sounds? Its vowel system has its own rules. Perhaps the commonest is the treatment of unmarked RP's *a* in *man* and *sat*, which bring them closer to 'men' and 'set'. In September 1939 Prime Minister Neville Chamberlain broadcast to the nation the declaration of war, speaking from what he called the "Kebinet" office. The *o* in *stones* may come out like 'stains'. The *ou* in *house* or *about*, whose history from Chaucer to Shakespeare and beyond was traced in the last chapter, becomes in the mouths of some speakers of marked RP, and royalty in particular, 'abite the hice'. By this rule *allowance* and *alliance* have the same sound. There is a whole range of words in which the simple *o*, as in *cost*, becomes *aw* (cawst): *off* (awf), *cloth* (clawth), with a similar treatment given to *cross, lost, froth*, etc. Barbara Woodhouse, a hugely successful dog training expert and television personality, once had to deal with a horse stuck in a *lawft*; and in the course of their long public careers both the Queen and the Queen Mother have given us examples such as *awfen* (often) and *awfer* (offer). The *ŏ* in words like *hope*, if it does not receive the 'hape' treatment, may get a very rounded form, and the short *o* in unstressed words like *to* can become 'ter'. The sounds represented by the spellings *i/y* or *a* at the ends of words can have their own special value, so that *army* might come out something like 'arm-air', and *India* 'Indi-ah'. Marked RP has its own way with certain standard English diphthongs: *tour* becoming 'tore', *fire* 'fah' (and I once heard an archbishop preach on the '*pah* of the British *empah*'). Thus *powerless* comes out the same as *parlous*; and *really* and *rarely*, words which are often used in opposing senses, are confusingly pronounced the same, while *shore/Shaw* cannot be distinguished from *sure*. In *comrade, Montgomery* and even *combat, om* is likely to become 'um'. For some speakers the *i* in *wine* comes out as in 'wane', but this may be only among the very 'refaned'. Every variety of every language develops its own distinctive way of fixing the positions of the jaw, lips, tongue, and other organs to produce its sounds (called technically 'articulatory set'). Marked RP tends to produce a very distinctive articulatory set, in which a 'stiff upper lip' may be a prominent feature, and may contribute to the fact that in the sentence 'I really have no idea' every single syllable may have a different sound for some marked RP speakers as compared with the unmarked RP speaker.

I say *some* marked RP speakers because it is necessary to emphasize that not all of them will use the entire range of variant forms available, and the use of the *aw* in the single example of *off*, for example, does not necessarily imply that the speaker's accent is marked rather than unmarked RP. Furthermore, there may be additional forms that identify marked RP speakers, since this type of accent is a feature of a complete upper-class dialect which has been in existence for hundreds of years, with elements of its own vocabulary, grammar, and idiom.

More than thirty years ago a linguistics professor, Alan S. C. Ross, co-operated with an English journalist of upper-class background, Nancy Mitford, to produce a book which popularized the terms 'U' and 'non-U', distinguishing genuine Upperclass speech forms from those which were not. Most of their concern was with vocabulary: napkin was U, serviette non-U; lavatory U, toilet non-U. It was non-U to say handbag rather than bag, or lounge rather than sitting-room, even radio rather than wireless. U-speakers simply did not say 'Pleased to meet you' on being introduced, nor did they refer to dying as 'passing on'. Ross and Mitford's concern was not so much with pronunciation in the generalized sense of accent, but rather with individual words such as *forehead*, whose non-U pronunciation follows the spelling but which U-speakers rhyme with *horrid*.

The U/non-U discussion aroused widespread interest at the time, and the terms are still in use, though the 1956 distinctions do not always apply, if indeed they ever did, for Ross and Mitford's account was light-hearted and highly impressionistic, its representativeness was doubtful, and it was never subjected to any kind of empirical research. To an extent, of course, this is true of some of the phenomena reported in this book, which often derive more from my own judgement and professional experience than from statistically verifiable experiments, and only deserve as much credence as they are granted by a consensus of well-informed opinion. The real point about Ross and Mitford is not whether they were right about every detail of the vocabulary, grammar, and idiom of the upper-class dialect of their generation, but their very plausible demonstration that such a dialect existed, alongside the distinctive accent which we have later come to identify as marked RP. Our interest lies in the fact that this twentieth-century manifestation was a lineal descendant of a much earlier phenomenon, which we can begin to identify as early as the sixteenth century and possibly even before that.

As we saw in Chapter Two, the standard English accent which had emerged by the early sixteenth century was associated with the highest social classes and with the most educated, and it was the process of formal education which made it more widely available. But already in the sixteenth century observers were finding it necessary to distinguish this standard form, spoken in governmental and other educated circles, from another accent which was also different from the non-standard accents of the mass of the population: the special and *affected* speech of members of the 'courtly' circle. It may also have been the case that the aristocracy of the fourteenth and fifteenth centuries, and their hangers-on in London, adopted affected forms of speech to increase their social distance from the lower classes.

What we can see at work here is a tendency, which is paralleled in many societies, for the upper classes to shelter behind a linguistic barrier that distinguishes them not only from the peasantry (who may in fact offer little competition or threat) but also from the rising middle classes and from the intelligentsia. In Russia for well over a century before 1917 this device was taken to extreme lengths: the great landed aristocratic families created just such a barrier around themselves by speaking the purest and most elegant Parisian French. For reasons which will become clear later, I will call any such special variety of language, associated not with the most highly educated but with those who are socially the most highly privileged, a HYPERLECT, remembering that this term can cover not just their accent (which in the case of contemporary Britain I have called 'marked RP') but may also refer to the complete range of accent, grammar, vocabulary, and idiom which constitute a social dialect.

In the plays of the Restoration period there are many instances of non-standard accents being used to poke fun at individuals' social origins, but in addition to the now common distinction between comic countryfolk and the more educated and sophisticated city-dwellers, there are also references to a third category: courtiers, social 'swells', and their hangers-on, who adopt an affected accent and sometimes other speech forms such as a drawl. The wealthy peer Lord Foppington (the very name is suggestive) in Sir John Vanbrugh's *The Relapse* (1696) regularly says *stap* for stop, *nine a'clack* (nine o'clock), washing my *mauth* (mouth), I *resalve* (resolve), *naw* (now), this *tawn* (town); and *pax* (pox), and, 'I am *nat* altogether so *fand* (fond) . . .'

Vanbrugh did not invent this form of pronunciation. We know of aristocratic figures from the second half of the seventeenth century like Robert, second Earl of Sunderland, a leading politician whose "drawling way" of speaking was quoted by a contemporary as a "very amusing specimen of the court pronunciation in the reign of Charles II". Sunderland's 'fashion' was to "distend" the vowels: "Whaat," said he, "if his maajesty taarn out faarty of us, may not he have faarty others to saarve him as well? And what matters who saarves his maajesty, so long as his maajesty is saarved?"

The hyperlect which can still be heard in socially privileged circles in twentieth-century Britain has been able to draw upon a number of forms of speech which have been regarded as affected, particular, conservative, or old-fashioned by commentators writing at various periods over the past two hundred years and more. In the nineteenth century many upper-class speakers used conservative pronunciations like *awficer* (officer), *yaller* (yellow) – Gladstone had both of these – *goold* (gold), and *cawfy* (coffee: a centenarian interviewed on BBC radio in 1961 used this form). *Obleege* for 'oblige' seems to have been upper class in the eighteenth century but sank to a more despised status in the nineteenth, and the same sort of development probably affected the pronunciation of *doo* (for due) and *dooty* (duty) which are nowadays expected only of Americans or speakers of certain English popular dialects, which may extend its use to the word 'bootiful'. A test of real social quality used to be the word *girl*: "The higher classes pronounce it as if it were spelt 'gairl' whereas the vulgar pronounce it as if it were spelt 'gurl'," wrote King William IV's granddaughter, the Countess of Munster, at the end of the nineteenth century, and this hyperlectal pronunciation of *girl*, as 'gairl' or 'gell', persisted well into our own day. There was a similarly arbitrary insistence on idiomatic forms such as 'going to *be* married' (rather than *get* married) and '*driving* in one's carriage' (rather than *riding*). If brashness was characteristic of the up-and-coming, those who had long since 'arrived' could advertise their modesty – even self-effacement – by replacing *I* or *me* by the impersonal 'one', such as is often heard from the Queen and Prince Charles today, and among the upper classes generally, especially among speakers of marked RP. A more surprising feature was the survival in the nineteenth-century hyperlect of verb forms which had long come to be regarded as non-standard, such as *you was, it don't matter, we ain't*, and *ain't it?*, all of which could be heard in the most aristocratic – even royal – households for well over a century after the Cambridge professor and poet Thomas Gray used such a form in prophesying that the illness of the Master of his college was temporary: "Dr Long will recover, mind if he *don't*." Such forms have passed out of upper-class speech in our own day, but there are still occasional echoes. Harold Macmillan, Prime Minister in 1957 (who died, as Earl of Stockton, in 1986 aged ninety-two) went to Eton in 1908 and then to Oxford. In a broadcast interview in 1981 he discussed the work of particular novelists who, he said, "achieve a certain flashy success – but it *don't* last."

The pronunciation of *h* in late nineteenth-century upper-class speech was complicated. As in modern speech, words like *hour, honour, heir* and *honest* were pronounced without the initial *h*, but this list was extended, for all educated speakers up until at least the middle of the nineteenth century, by dropping the *h* in *hospital, herb, home* (in some contexts, e.g. *at home*), and *hotel*: all his life Winston Churchill said *at 'ome* and *an 'otel*; and there are still socially privileged speakers today who use these forms. Like Churchill, the actor Sir John Gielgud begins the words *humour* and *humorous* with the sound *yu*. Upper-class speech also tolerated the dropping of the *h* in the pronouns *him* and *her, his* and *hers*, in certain contexts where from other speakers this would have been stigmatized. All RP speakers tend, in informal speech, to reduce the degree of aspiration they give to the *h* at the beginning of a word that is weakly stressed in a sentence, but in the hyperlect this tendency was taken to its extreme, and there are traces of this in the launching speech of the Queen Mother (born 1900), "May God bless 'er and all who sail in 'er", and even in the accent of her grandson Prince Charles, as when he read the lesson at the Falklands Memorial service in Llandaff Cathedral in 1982: "And all the trumpets sounded for 'im on the other side." A shortening of the pronoun *them* to *'em* used also to be permissible in this social dialect.

An even better-known charactertistic was the substitution of the suffix *-in* for *-ing*, made famous in the phrase *huntin' and shootin'*, which was typical of many speakers. The headmasters of Eton whose reigns spanned the years 1868 to 1905, Hornby and Warre, both used the *-in* form. Warre thundered in the chapel pulpit against the evils of "bettin' and gamblin' ". In his memoirs the Oxford scholar Sir Maurice Bowra wrote of his acquaintance early this century with Mrs Maud Yorke, the aristocratic wife of a banker: "She talked the clipped language of her time and class", which not only involved "dropping the -g" from words like *huntin'* and *shootin'*, and in the terms *brushin' room* and *goin's-on among the servants*, but she also "managed somehow to drop it from words which did not contain it, as in Cheltin'ham and Chippin'ham".

This account cannot do justice to the enormous variety of 'old fashioned' vocabulary, idiom, grammar, and pronunciation from which, from decade to decade, members of the social elite selected forms which set them apart from other people. Throughout the nineteenth and early twentieth centuries *Punch* made frequent satirical references to the latest manifestations of these. From time to time the fashion required speakers, as in the days of the second Earl of Sunderland, to drawl. (There are exponents of this speaking style even today, the best-known perhaps being the broadcaster and influential *Observer* columnist Katherine Whitehorn.) Regional influence and personal idiosyncrasies also made their contribution to the hyperlect; either of these may have been the determinant of the distinctive accent of the great Lord Curzon, Viceroy of India and Foreign Secretary, "prototype in the popular imagination of the aloof and pompous English aristocrat", who came so close to becoming Prime Minister in 1923. In his reported instructions regarding an offending paperweight on his first day at the Foreign Office, Curzon's short *a*s (as in *cat*) were the opposite if the *a*s affected by the Earl of Sunderland: "Remove that object of *glass* and *brass* and bring me one of *alabaster*."

The novelist George Eliot referred in *Felix Holt* (1866) to the aristocracy's "refined high-bred tone and accent", but readers of my account of some of the main characteristics of that accent will already have noticed two disconcerting things about it. The first is that some of its features are strikingly similar to ones that are also characteristic of the most disparaged dialects of the lower classes. *Awff, clawth, crawss*, and so on take us straight back to the Cockney speech of Eliza Doolittle. Ending a word *-in* rather than *-ing* was – and still is – a feature of many nonstandard regional dialects, and learning when to pronounce *h-* at the beginning of a word, and when not, had by the middle of the nineteenth century become one of the vital distinctions between the educated and the uneducated. Yet here we have an upper-class dialect which plays fast and loose with *h-*: in fact, it operates a completely different set of rules for when it is to be pronounced at the beginning of a word and when not, which effectively differentiates the hyperlect not only from the *h-* rules of the lower classes, but also from those which the middle classes have imbibed from their parents or painstakingly acquired at school. We can better understand how there could be striking points of similarity between the accent of the aristocrat and that of his lowliest tenants and servants when we reflect that the social gap between them was so wide, and so clearly expressed by a thousand other aspects of life – including clothing, physique, and even smell – that to share a number of speech forms with them implied no kind of threat to the aristocrat's status. Moreover, these shared forms were outnumbered by all the other differences of pronunciation (as, for example, in *girl*). The pretensions of the rising middle classes, on the other hand, *were* a potential threat, and it was in this respect that the nuances of the hyperlect provided such an effective barrier.

Compared with standard English as spoken with a standard accent, which had an army of teachers to teach it, the hyperlect could only be acquired by direct and extended social experience in the right circles. It could be absorbed by attendance at a select number of very famous and expensive boarding schools, like Eton and Winchester, and at a few colleges at Cambridge and Oxford, especially if one obtained access to the right social 'set'. Even at schools like Eton the learning process required especially sensitive discrimination, since, in the matter of *h-* at least, there were masters on the staff in the second half of the nineteenth century who variously represented the hyperlectal rules for *h-* and the stigmatized *h-* rules of a regional accent (in this particular case, Yorkshire). In one of Tom Sharpe's comic novels, *Riotous Assembly* (1971), set in South Africa, there is a revealing description of how in Victorian times the British had imposed an "immutable sense of hierarchy" on the social life of a garrison town in colonial Natal:

> Viceroys, governors, generals, down the rank swept, broadening as they went, through nuances too subtle to enumerate, where schools, and wives' fathers' professions, and *a dropped aspirate* or one *retained -g* could cause a major to step, in an instant, up above a lieutenant-colonel.

The second surprising and disconcerting fact about this upper-class accent is how 'affected' and even ridiculous some of its forms sound to us, as indeed they sounded to large numbers of its hearers in past centuries. Its own speakers presumably did not sound ridiculous to each other, and in any case the adverse reaction of the rest of the world – which was not normally expressed to their faces – was a small price to pay for the advantages of a social dialect which excluded outsiders, and served as a badge of their own rank as effectively as any coat of arms.

The Second World War has frequently been cited as a great leveller of social class divisions, with people working closely together whose backgrounds would not otherwise have given them to expect even to speak to each other. The Mitfords – the second Lord Redesdale's six daughters and a son, born around the turn of the century – were brought up in their Cotswold home to speak with a hyperlectal accent spiced with idiosyncratic family forms, and their "similarity in voice and feature" to one another was a matter of comment. The Hon. Deborah Mitford, who went on to become a duchess, wrote to her sister the Hon. Diana (Lady Mosley) in January 1944 of her own contribution to the war effort: "I do disgusting work now, do feel sorry for me. It's in the YWCA canteen and it's very embarrassing because they all copy my voice." Another sister, the Hon. Nancy Mitford – whose later collaboration with Alan S. C. Ross in the attempted description of aspects of this 'U' dialect we have already noted – got an even more pointed reaction to her accent. She had taken up fire-watching, which she enjoyed hugely, and was invited to give lectures on the subject to trainees. Then the invitations suddenly stopped, and the organizers explained in some embarrassment, "It's your accent. It irritates people so much they'd like to put *you* on the fire."

Other forms of a privileged social dialect were in existence by 1900 which augmented RP by a range of special vocabulary and idiom. Every major public school, for example, developed its own special language requiring intensive induction courses, and even oral examinations, for new boys: Winchester's was notoriously elaborate. By the turn of the century the special forms among the various individual schools had enough in common for it to be possible to speak of a generalized public school slang which was mediated to a wider public by the huge industry of novels and stories about public school life. Cambridge and Oxford universities were already by the 1850s "the hotbeds of fashionable slang", which was enriched towards the end of the century by forms which reflected the new strength of 'public school consciousness' at those two universities in that period. One form which was typical of public school speech and also that of the ancient universities (particularly Oxford) between the 1880s and around 1940 was the word formation which added *-er* or *-ers* to a base which included the stressed syllable of the word: rugby (football) became *rugger*, association football *soccer*, congratulations became *gratters*, breakfast *brekker*. This form survives as somewhat self-conscious slang in a few current words like champers (champagne) and starkers (stark naked) and is still used in coining nicknames for England cricketers. Among the public schoolboys and Oxford undergraduates whose speech it dominated by around 1900, it was extended to many personal names, and also gave rise to many exotic forms such as *wagger-pagger-bagger* (waste-paper basket).

A further group which cultivated elaborate speech distinctions were the cadets at elite officer-training colleges for the army and navy, like Sandhurst, Woolwich, and Dartmouth. Here the distinctions were mainly of accent: extreme forms of marked RP which, though they may have sounded ludicrous in themselves to the men over whom these officers would serve, fulfilled the important function of emphasizing social distance and the cohesion of the officer group, and thus enhancing authority. In radio and TV interviews nowadays with kings and generals from foreign countries who as young men were sent to undergo officer training at Sandhurst, it is still common to hear traces of this accent.

Neither this, nor the more general form of the hyperlect heard among the English upper classes, was the type of accent to which millions of ordinary people – especially as they became more educated – have aspired for more than a century, if not for themselves then at least for their children. The pioneer of English phonetics, A. J. Ellis, wrote in 1869 of how "anxious and willing the social inferior is to adopt the pronunciation of the superiorly educated, if he can but learn it." Mechanisms for achieving such learning became available on a wide scale within a few years of Ellis's writing, as schools first for the privileged and then for the masses made feasible the ambition to 'talk proper'. But 'talking proper' did not necessarily mean the same as 'talking posh': the real 'lah-di-dah' voices and 'cut-glass' accents were restricted to persons of the very highest social privilege of birth or education, and to the relatively small number of those who had special reason to want to imitate them.

FOUR

Are some accents better than others?

A visitor on a tour of Britain today will encounter a bewildering variety of accents. A standard textbook introducing students to the subject of English accents and dialects uses, in addition to RP, ten examples of varieties of speech (especially accent): London Cockney; Norwich (East Anglia); Bristol (the west of England); South Wales; West Midlands (including Birmingham); Bradford (Yorkshire); Liverpool (Merseyside); Newcastle-upon-Tyne (the north-east); Edinburgh (Scotland); and Belfast (Northern Ireland).

Dr John Wells's massively detailed and scholarly three-volume study, *Accents of English* (1982) devotes its second volume to the British Isles. Apart from RP (in which he recognizes the upper-class form as well as the mainstream variety) he concentrates on three regions of England – London Cockney; the South of England (the Home Counties, East Anglia, and the West Country); and the North: "about half of the English speak with some degree of northern accent". The North in this sense includes parts of the Midlands, especially the Birmingham-Wolverhampton (West Midlands) conurbation, Leicester, and Peterborough. It also includes the 'typical' northern accents of the present counties of Greater Manchester, West Yorkshire, and South Yorkshire, and the distinctive accents of, for example, Tyneside (Geordie), Lancashire and Merseyside (whose purest Liverpool form is called 'Scouse'). He treats separately the accents of Wales, Scotland, and Ireland. Though since 1921 only Northern Ireland (Ulster) has been part of Britain, we also have plenty of opportunity to hear the accents of Southern Ireland (Eire) in the speech of those many of our fellow citizens on this side of the Irish Sea who originate from Eire.

The English accents of the inhabitants of Wales, Scotland, and Ireland (both Northern and Southern) are influenced by the original languages which are still spoken as mother tongues by a small proportion in those countries: in Ulster the accent is further complicated by the strong influence of Scots English. Welshmen normally recognize two main types of Welsh accent – North Welsh and South Welsh, with many fine distinctions of each. Scotland has a great variety of Scottish English accents: some of them are readily intelligible to speakers of RP and to American visitors, but others are exceptionally difficult to understand for such outsiders and even for some speakers from different parts of Scotland. Some Northern Ireland accents can also be hard for outsiders to understand, for example the working-class speech of Belfast, and some rural Ulster accents in which, for example, they may pronounce 'nothing' as *neeth'n* and say *hworr* for 'where'.

An additional complication in the accents picture results from the immigration into Britain of large numbers of people from the West Indies from the 1950s onwards, and of Asians from East Africa and the Indian subcontinent over the same period, especially in the 1970s. The fact that most West Indians came speaking a mixture of Creole and standard English "which is neither one thing nor the other", making it "a language on its own and foreign to English", has, according to West Indian community leaders, led to widespread misunderstanding and consequent disadvantage for West Indian children. In a similar way, the failure to acknowledge the very real differences between the pronunciation of Indian English and standard English (see Chapter Six) has led to many misunderstandings and avoidable hurts.

Amid this profusion of accents which are distinctive of regions, or of social classes within those regions, certain facts stand out. The great majority of the people of Britain do not speak RP, though all of them understand this variety of accent because they hear it as the form most commonly used on radio and television and from public figures. A very large proportion, certainly the majority, of the population do not conform exactly to the grammar of standard English in their informal speech, though people tend towards it more when they write; again, they are confronted with standard grammar on most radio and TV broadcasts, in films, newspapers, magazines, and books.

But even if it is true, as has been roughly estimated, that as few as 3 per cent of the population actually speak with an RP accent themselves (and only a tiny fraction of these can be expected to use marked RP forms), nevertheless RP has exercised a great influence over many English speakers. Two factors – education and social class – operate to support the generalization of which we will be frequently reminded: that the higher a person's social-class standing, or alternatively the greater the length of someone's formal education, the greater the likelihood that he or she will speak RP or a form of accent fairly close to it, and that other dialect features, such as grammar and vocabulary, will be similarly influenced.

Specialists in the study of language have developed a useful terminology to describe this phenomenon of degrees of difference between speech varieties. The term ACROLECT describes the dialect (or accent) which is accorded highest prestige: in British English the accent concerned in this category is, as we have seen, RP. The 'broadest' form of popular speech is called the BASILECT. In 1850, the majority of people in rural areas, especially those with least education, spoke a basilect: those forms survive now among "elderly people with little education" (as one scholar puts it) in rather isolated areas. With every year that passes, fewer and fewer young children are introduced to the meanings of the old dialect words, and the accents of more

Accents

(H)	Acrolect	Mesolect	Basilect
	RP (BBC news reader)	most Britons	historic, 'broadest' forms

← — — — — — — — — — — — —

education

and more of them move to at least an intermediate stage in the direction of RP, which is called the MESOLECT.

We have already noted one additional refinement needed to fit these categories to the British accent picture in the twentieth century: the line should be extended leftwards to acknowledge that special form of RP associated with the very highest category of social privilege and not accessible to the majority by means of education, which in the previous chapter I labelled the HYPERLECT. The arrow again reminds us of the prime responsibility of education in causing speakers of regional and lower-class accents to adapt their own speech to RP or something very close to it. How close, and how far that arrow extends leftwards, is a subject we will return to later.

All round the world, in most cultures and language groups, the way individuals speak provides clues about their geographical origin, social status, age, sex, occupation, even personal dispositions and attitudes. Some of the indicators of this kind of information are beyond the control of the individual concerned: for example old people's voices are distinguishable from twenty-five-year-olds' voices, and so are toddlers'. Women do not choose the pitch ranges which, in general, distinguish their voices from men's. There is evidence, though, that within the normal biological range of adult male, adult female, or boyish voice, the particular range exploited by any of these voices will vary between cultures and language groups. It is said, for example, that American males, as a group, tend to have deeper voices, and I have heard this claimed also for German males. Boy sopranos in English cathedral choirs produce a very different quality of sound from their counterparts in Christian regions of the Middle East.

We have already seen that speaking the marked form of RP requires a different setting of the jaw, lips, and other speech organs from speaking mainstream (unmarked) RP. Another set of such differences operates among speakers of many regional and social accents. These distinctive uses of certain speech organs to produce the sounds which characterize the local accent are learned socially in childhood, then become habitual. It has been suggested that the distinctive voice quality, as well as the distinctive vowels and consonants, of Liverpool Scouse relate to the prevalence of adenoid problems in that city. I have also heard it suggested that the Glaswegian accent developed among speakers with ill-fitting false teeth; and others have pointed to the possibility that workers in industrial environments heavily polluted by fumes may have developed understandable tendencies not to open their mouths fully, or the habit of speaking from one side of the mouth, with predictable effects on their diction.

In many societies, including contemporary Britain, voice quality, especially pitch (which, we have seen, is largely not a matter of personal choice) significantly affects the way people's personalities are evaluated by others. The ideal voice from this point of view is a rich, fruity baritone, and everybody knows of men in public life, or among their own friends, who have benefitted from the accident of having developed this kind of voice in adolescence. I can think of at least one bishop in the Church of England in recent years whose effectiveness as a speaker relied heavily on the fruity quality of his voice; much the same was true of the late politician, Lord Boothby. Indeed, W. F. Deedes, the then editor of the *Daily Telegraph*, underlined my point in his sympathetic obituary tribute to Boothby in 1986, when he quoted a House of Commons discussion on herrings: "With that *rich throaty* voice, riffling his fingers through his hair, he made herrings sound *thrilling*."

An important ingredient in the success of Gilbert Harding, the popular radio and television personality of the 1950s and 1960s, was his voice. By contrast the author H. G. Wells and the great English cricketer W. G. Grace are said to have had high, even squeaky voices: fortunately the activities which made them famous did not depend on the favourable evaluation of their voices. Part of the attractiveness of the speech of actors like Sir John Gielgud, the late Richard Burton, and Sir James Mason may be the resonant qualities which their vocal styles have exploited. How much success as screen actors would Orson Welles or Lee Marvin have enjoyed if they had had high-pitched or piping voices? Interestingly, this factor is not confined to human beings: it is reported in the mating behaviour both of toads and of deer!

The actor Charles Laughton was perhaps the supreme example of a career built upon a voice. "At the peak of his powers," claims the film critic George Perry, "he could assert an intense, compelling presence that would eclipse all others near him." Yet this power had nothing whatever to do with his personal appearance, which could charitably be described as 'unprepossessing': Laughton described his own face as being "like an elephant's behind". Perry identifies Laughton's essential strength:

> Laughton's voice was hypnotic. It was not strong – he had been gassed in Flanders – but abundant texture, shading and feeling more than compensated. Words became magical when he uttered them.

Perry describes how, during pauses in the making of his films, Laughton would hold groups of unsophisticated American film technicians spellbound by reciting passages from the Bible, or Lincoln's Gettysburg Address. On another occasion he successfully responded to a challenge from Ed Sullivan on television to recite an insurance document in such a way as to make it sound fascinating.

Voices like Laughton's are rare, however, and many men of worth have been less influential than their talents merited because of the arbitrary distribution of such vocal qualities. As *The Times* obituarist of a Scottish church leader put it in 1985:

Had his voice matched the sweep and relevance of his thought, and the felicitous character of his language, his fame as a preacher would have been country-wide.

All these vocal features are ones over which the individual has very little control. Accent, however, is a different matter, since although we do not choose the accent which we grow up speaking, we can alter it to a considerable extent. In fact, everybody's accent changes, at least slightly, in the course of a lifetime. It changes according to the style of what we are saying, especially in relation to the degree of formality or informality of the occasion. And it often changes in relation to the accent of the person to whom we are speaking. We all recognize the phenomenon of the 'telephone voice', which may contain very different features from our normal accent. My students describe my own accent as unmarked RP, which is a fair reflection of the kind (and length) of education I received, but I possess a tape-recording of an interview I conducted a few years ago with an elderly titled lady, and my children have pointed out with glee that in it I respond to her accent by using many forms which I have described in the previous chapter as characteristic of the marked (or 'posh', hyperlectal) variety.

What evidence is there, beyond reported impressions of prejudice, about the way people in Britain react, more than seventy years after Bernard Shaw's Eliza Doolittle, to different regional and social accents, and to RP in its different forms? From the 1960s onwards, some fairly systematic experiments have been performed which have helped us to build a general picture of the overall pattern of the way accents are evaluated in this country. Many of the experiments are based on a technique devised originally in Canada to test the way people there react to French and to English accents respectively. Various audiences are confronted with passages spoken in different accents, and asked to judge them, from sound alone, in terms of a list of qualities such as intelligent, hard-working, friendly, etc. In the form in which it is generally administered, this method of evaluation excludes or minimizes factors that would complicate listeners' reactions, such as the speaker's gender and voice quality (the 'Charles Laughton' effect), etc., by using actors skilled in speaking authentically a whole range of different accents. Whatever reservations one might have about this type of experiment – and I would have several – the fact remains that the picture revealed, over a considerable number of tests with audiences taken from different samples of the population, shows a very high degree of consistency, which is further confirmed by other, more informal, experiments based on speakers who use their own natural accents.

This is the general picture that emerges. The overwhelming majority of the hundreds of individuals tested in different parts of the country, and themselves speakers of many varieties of English accent, rated RP as the most favoured accent on such criteria as communicative effectiveness, social status, and above all pleasantness of sound: RP is often referred to by those tested as being 'nicer', 'more pleasant', 'more beautiful' than other accents, and the term 'well-spokenness' is used most often of RP speakers.

All other British accents have less prestige than RP, but they are not equal in their relative inferiority to it. There is a hierarchy of accents in which RP always has the top position, and the descending order of acceptability, though it varies slightly in different parts of the country, tends to reflect the following pattern. Next after RP are the most educated varieties of Scottish

English accent, and also near the top are the corresponding educated accents of Wales and Ireland. After that there is a broad cluster of English provincial accents such as 'northern' English (with Yorkshire generally high) and the West Country; some samples also put Tyneside Geordie in the higher reaches of this 'middling' category.

With depressing regularity, four accents compete for bottom place: London (Cockney), Liverpool (Scouse), Glaswegian*, and the West Midlands accent especially associated with Birmingham. When Northern Ireland accents are included in the experiment, Belfast tends to join this most disparaged category.

Indian accents in English are rated fairly low and so, generally, are West Indian accents. In those tests where the marked form of RP has been separately identified, it has been given a rating lower than mainstream RP, and in some respects very much lower. Given the reservation that in many of the tests it is difficult to be confident that non-standard accents *of equal breadth* are being compared, it is fairly clear that speakers with mild or slight degrees of accent are more highly rated than those with really broad non-standard accents.

Since no single experiment has compared the evaluation of *all* of the hundreds of identifiable accents of the United Kingdom, or even just of England (the task becomes logistically difficult to set up for more than about a dozen at a time), there is least certainty about the relative positions of the accents in the middle band. But as to who fills those top and bottom positions, there seems to be unanimous agreement that the unmarked RP represented by most BBC newsreaders is accorded the highest

---

* The 'Glasgow accent' covers a wide spectrum of varieties, from the most educated to the "gutter-Glasgow" of the streets, associated by one Glasgow teacher with "drunks and women shouting". Features regarded as 'typical Glaswegian' include a ferociously rolled *r*; a regular glottal stop for *t*, both in the middle of the word (as in *butter*) and at the end (*but*); numerous vowel changes, such as commonly give *down* a sound like 'doen' and make *about* come out like RP's 'a boot'; and the word *no* becoming *nae*.

prestige and regarded as the most pleasing to listen to, while four specific accents which are associated with the speech of the common people in particular conurbations in Scotland, the North of England, the Midlands and the capital city itself, are deemed 'extremely unpleasant' and 'ugly'. One of the most staggering findings of all is the extent to which these attitudes of respect for RP, and the readiness to stigmatize certain other accents, are shared by great numbers of *the speakers of those stigmatized varieties themselves*.

These experiments also show that not only do the many listeners sampled accord highest prestige to the RP accent, they also attribute to RP speakers a long catalogue of favourable attributes. A speaker of RP is held to rate more highly than the speakers of all other varieties on the following qualities:

> intelligence
> ambition
> leadership
> self-confidence
> wealth
> occupational status

and even – amazing though it may seem – good looks, tallness, and cleanliness. Though the speakers of all varieties of other than RP are considered not to be able to compete with RP speakers in the above characteristics, they are often rated more highly than RP speakers on the following:

> friendliness/good-naturedness
> generosity, kind-heartedness
> honesty, integrity
> sense of humour.

But even these concessions do not always hold true: there have been tests in which speakers of the most disparaged accents (like Cockney) are rated negatively even by such speakers themselves in respect of friendliness and kindness, compared with RP speakers. The quality 'hardworking' is one about which evaluations disagree, with some listeners associating it more with RP voices and others crediting it more to speakers with non-standard accents. Likewise, 'reliability' or 'trustworthiness' is viewed ambivalently. Some listeners give the least favourable ratings in the category, "Would you buy a second-hand car from this man?" (i.e. a man with this accent) to speakers with Cockney and Liverpool accents. Other listeners tested claim to find RP speakers 'unreliable' or 'untrustworthy': in some cases this seems to be because they detect that the speaker has adapted from a non-standard accent to RP, and need reassurance about his motives for doing so. What is also common to such studies is that when listeners are asked to assign occupations to tape-recorded voices, professional jobs (such as lawyer or bank manager) are only assigned to RP voices, while Liverpool and Cockney voices are matched with jobs like greengrocer and chimney-sweep.

Other researches suggest that a standard accent can enhance the credibility of a defendant or witness in a court case, and may not only be crucial to the outcome of a job interview – which will surprise no one – but even influence the kind of diagnosis a patient will receive from his doctor.

Despite the variable scientific reliability of the experiments referred to, the unanimity of their main findings makes it difficult to disregard the general picture which emerges, which puts the RP accent in a position of unchallengeable prestige, earning its speakers all kinds of favourable assumptions about intelligence, competence, and drive (and causing a number of other positive, but patently irrational, attributes to attach to them also). Next to (unmarked) RP are a number of accents associated with 'nationality', like Scots, Welsh and Irish, whose relative standing is helped by three factors which also affect the positioning of the provincial accents in the middle band between RP at the top and the most unpopular accents at the bottom. These three factors, which are closely interrelated, all serve to make certain non-standard accents more highly rated than others. The first is the breadth of the accent: as we have seen, slight or moderate accents are more favourably perceived than broad ones. The second is the extent to which the accent is perceived as being an indicator of the quality of educatedness in the speaker. The third factor is one we will call rusticity: non-standard accents which are traditionally associated with rural areas seem to be more highly rated than those associated with large industrial cities. The 'Educated Scottish Standard English' spoken by many people in Edinburgh is a good example of a combination of these factors. Within Scotland it is rated at least as high as RP, and in certain respects (which will be discussed later) even higher. In England an Edinburgh accent comes close to RP in prestige ratings, combining as it does the associations of educatedness (Edinburgh has a fine university and a large professional class, and its architecture reflects a rich culture); its degree of mildness compared with many other Scottish accents; and the fact that, though not exactly rustic, Edinburgh benefits scenically from comparisons with Glasgow which is the centre of an ugly, sprawling industrial conurbation.

It is debatable how far the existence of such a hierarchy of accents, a descending order of prestige between a most-favoured acrolect at the top and a set of heavily stigmatized accents at the bottom, is a situation unique to Britain. It is often commented that in countries like West Germany and France a variety of accents serves to reveal people's diverse geographical origins, but not to fasten upon them a whole set of social advantages and disadvantages as happens here. This may be broadly true, but it is not the whole story. In West Germany, for example, the accents of certain regions tend to be made fun of, and whereas a politician with, say, a Swabian accent might achieve high office in his native region, this might reduce his chances of being taken seriously as a candidate for office at national level. In France there are all kinds of jokes about particular regional accents, and a French academic once told me that when teaching English at a famous lycée in Paris he conducted all his lessons in English, whenever possible, so as to avoid using his normal (French regional) accent which his sophisticated pupils tended to mock as provincial. When a princess of the Dutch royal house recently married a commoner, it is rumoured that he was given strong encouragement to lose his disparaged Rotterdam accent. Even so, in none of these continental countries is the stigma of a non-standard accent as penetrating as it appears to be in Britain.

How are we to explain the existence of this distinctively British accent hierarchy and the relative placings of specific accents within it? Most people, when asked why they favour some accents and disfavour others, justify this by using terms such as 'the most pleasant', 'the most beautiful', and the notion that this hierarchy represents a scale of beauty of sound has a very long history. The classic twentieth-century encapsulation of this argument was made in 1934 by H. C. Wyld, a great historian of the English language, himself a product of a leading public school, who had become a professor at Oxford. Wyld claimed that, if given the chance to compare every vowel sound in RP with the corresponding sounds in non-standard accents, no unbiased observer would hesitate to prefer RP "as the most pleasing and sonorous form".

Certainly the way in which Shaw represented Eliza Doolittle's accent (and her father's) seems to have been intended to emphasize the ugliness of the sound. We have already noted (see page 29) how, barely six years before *Pygmalion*, London teachers and others mounted an attack on Cockney's *unpleasant twang*. In the 1980s a woman listener who took part in an evaluation experiment on accents and who found much to admire in certain non-standard ones, explained that even though she had been a great fan of the Beatles, the Scouse accent had always "got on her nerves". Speakers with strong Glaswegian accents often themselves make comments implying that they consider that the standard English accent "sounds nicer".

So it is probably true to say that most people who comment

on differences between standard and non-standard accents believe that the basis of their judgements is aesthetic – a matter of taste such as distinguishes a good piece of music from a bad one, a good painting from a daub, a good poem from a piece of meretricious verse. But we must express some reservations about accepting the claims frequently made for the aesthetic basis of accent judgements. Take the case of Cockney. Many people say that the Cockney vowel system which turns the phrase 'make or break' into 'mike or brike', and 'I' and 'my' into 'Oi' and 'moi' produces sounds which are ugly. But both these 'Cockneyfied' sounds exist in RP, even if they are used in other words. The Cockney pronunciation of 'basin' is almost identical to RP's *bison*, and who has claimed that the sound of *bison* is ugly? RP's 'ties' becomes Cockney's *toys*, but *toys* already exists as a perfectly respectable-sounding RP word. Cockney's replacement of *th* by either *v* or *f*, as appropriate, (*wiv* for with, *fings* for things) produces words like *fin* (thin) and *free* (three) which already exist (though with a different meaning) in RP. The true Cockney is supposed to pronounce 'mouth' as *marf*. The *-arf* sound, which critics claim to dislike, already exists in RP's *scarf, half, daft, laughter* and many more words. In fact most of the individual sounds which are distinctive of all the non-standard accents of England, especially the most disparaged ones, already exist in RP. Why should they suddenly become ugly when they appear in another context?

Further doubt is cast on the notion that non-standard accents are inherently offensive to the canons of good taste in matters of sound, when we look at experiments in which outsiders who either speak another world variety of English (for example North Americans), or have a totally different mother tongue but have learned excellent English, fail to detect the ugliness or unpleasantness of sound which citizens of Britain are all so ready to assign to some non-RP accents.

Neither of these arguments is, however, conclusive. The fact that many individual sounds which are said to be ugly in, say,

Cockney are judged pleasant in RP may be misleading: perhaps it is only from a *general pattern* composed of a number of sounds and their relation to each other, that we form aesthetic judgements about what is pleasant or ugly. And aesthetic judgements are notoriously limited in their validity. What is regarded as beautiful in one country's music may be a mere sequence of discordant sounds to the citizens of another country, and the reactions of Americans or Frenchmen to non-standard English accents perhaps have little authority in judging whether *within the culture of Britain itself* these criteria of pleasant or ugly sounds are as genuine a foundation as they are claimed to be for the evaluation of different British accents.

Even so, I remain highly sceptical of the explanation that the hierarchy of accents is due ultimately to the inherent beauty or otherwise of the sound system of different varieties. This is because I perceive another factor at work which I think is much more powerful in determining our reaction to accents. This is the tendency, which now pervades the whole of our society, for us to attach to particular accents certain generalized assumptions about the values and attributes considered typical of certain social groups. In other words, we judge accents by stereotypes which we already have about their speakers.

Many theorists use a version of this 'association of ideas' theory to argue as follows. RP is the accent which has become associated with the 'ruling classes', the 'establishment', the highest levels of power and prestige. It is spoken by those who are at the top in social, political, and economic terms, and they exploit its special standing in order to keep themselves at the top. All other varieties of accent are downgraded in comparison with it, and the speakers of even the most disfavoured accents have come to adopt this rating scale which combines respect for RP with devaluation of their own accents. They do this either because they genuinely admire the power and prestige which are associated with RP, or, more commonly, because they have been "brainwashed" to an extent which makes it "very unlikely" that they can evaluate accents "objectively". Teachers are cited as important agents of this "brainwashing process".

But we have already seen one flaw in the detail of this argument. Many of the most important members of the British 'establishment' do not speak with the most highly rated accent (mainstream RP), but instead tend to use what we have called marked RP. At the pinnacle of social prestige in Britain is the royal family, every detail of whose lives is made the subject of close public scrutiny. Yet the sovereign, the Queen Mother, and the heir to the throne all speak a variant of RP which is not the most widely admired or imitated accent – indeed in the mouths of other speakers it is actually ridiculed – nor is it anywhere formally taught. Members of many other categories enjoy very high prestige in Britain: political figures, media celebrities, famous footballers and cricketers, and pop stars. Nobody suggests that this enormous prestige, or the wealth and status which often comes with it, are connected with the fact that they all speak mainstream RP (which they clearly don't) or that their fame will have any long-term effect in establishing the particular non-standard accents some of them may have as a potential rival to RP as the main national model.

Pop singers seem to be the only possible exception to this generalization. There was a brief period when Liverpool Scouse became fashionable among young people because of the Beatles, but this quickly passed and Scouse resumed its place among the most stigmatized accents. Indeed, the most famous of the surviving Beatles, Paul McCartney, now commonly uses an accent which is barely distinguishable from RP. It does seem to be the case that the popularity associated with certain forms of music *can* affect people's linguistic behaviour: pop music has motivated millions of young people world-wide to learn English; and in America the specific genre known as 'country' music is said to have helped since 1945 to spread the 'Sunbelt' accent from the Appalachian Mountains into areas all over Middle America. It may be that one of the main influences on the speech of young people in Britain today, and even possibly an influence on the way RP itself has been changing slightly over recent years, is the 'mid-Atlantic' flavour of the accents in which many pop singers and pop music presenters speak or sing. While this may constitute a challenge to the national prestige of RP (or affect RP's main ingredients), what it does *not* do is affect the 'negative prestige' of the existing non-standard accents of Britain, especially the four most disfavoured ones.

So our objection to the common argument that the high rating of RP is due to its association with the social prestige deriving from economic and political power must be that it hits the wrong target. We need not quarrel with the 'association of ideas' argument, which says that certain values and attributes tend to get attached to particular accents, and that these assumptions come to affect every level of society, to the extent that even the speakers who are belittled by those assumptions come to accept them. The real question is: exactly which values and attributes are being ascribed to which accents? If it is not the prestige of economic, social, and political power, or even that of being a media celebrity, which dignifies RP, and their absence which devalues non-standard accents, then what is it?

The lists of qualities which listeners attribute respectively to RP speakers and to those with non-standard accents, in the evaluation experiments described on page 60, give us a clue. Setting aside the less credible ones ('good looks', 'cleanliness' etc.), the common threads running through the qualities most often cited (intelligence, self-confidence, occupational status, etc.) are associations in a general way with *educatedness* and with *competence*, especially competence in sophisticated tasks involving the possession of detailed knowledge and a wide range of uses of language. The attributes ascribed to the speakers of non-standard accents also have two common threads: *sociability* and *solidarity* (friendliness, humour, kind-heartedness to others, etc.).

We should not be surprised at the high value placed on

educatedness and competence in a modern technological society where so many elements of our economy, and of our lifestyle generally, relate to the ability to process knowledge accurately and to communicate in forms readily understandable by large numbers of people. Even the least educated members of society benefit from these skills in others and rely on finding them in the doctors, solicitors, and other professionals they consult; indeed they regard their accents as some kind of symbol of such educatedness and competence. These sought-after qualities are not symbolized exclusively by RP: there is a range of other accents which are compatible with educatedness. This is supremely true, for example, of certain Scottish accents (including, as we have seen, the Edinburgh one), spoken by large numbers of respected doctors, scientists, engineers, academics, and others who for well over a century have 'colonized' many professional occupations in England. In these cases their perceived educatedness can even compensate for a degree of breadth of accent which, in a speaker of a less educated variety, would lead to reactions which could prejudice his or her professional effectiveness. In Wales, where, in contrast to Scotland, many people in the course of extended education move to RP with few traces of a Welsh accent, it is nevertheless still possible to reconcile 'educatedness' with a noticeable Welsh accent, because of the long existence of a local Welsh intelligentsia of teachers, doctors, academics, and clergymen – again, many of these have 'colonized' the relevant professions in England. Similarly, in both Northern and Southern Ireland a regional accent is fully compatible with high professional status, provided it is that variety which is deemed to be 'educated'.

When we look at the rest of the accents of Britain, however – and let us here look particularly at England – we find that some non-standard accents are thought to be compatible with the attribute 'educatedness' while others are not. A Yorkshireman, a Mancunian, a Westcountryman may speak with a regional accent – provided it is not too broad – and no one will feel disposed to challenge his educatedness on the grounds of his accent alone. Yet a London Cockney, a Scouse speaker from Liverpool, a speaker of "Brum" (the Birmingham accent) as well as a typical Glaswegian and even, I have heard it said, a typical speaker of the Belfast accent, is denied that assumption of educatedness which would otherwise lift the stigma which, right across the nation, devalues his accent and the words he speaks in it.

It has been claimed, of course, that the obvious reason for this special dislike of these four accents (or, if Belfast is included, five) is a reflection of class prejudice, since they are all essentially working-class accents. This may be true, but it does not explain why the working-class accent in other parts of England, like the West Country, or Yorkshire, is not stigmatized to the same degree. A plausible reason is that the five stigmatized accents are especially, even exclusively, identified with the lower classes, whereas the Yorkshire or West Country accent is fairly strongly represented in middle-class speech as well. Plenty of prosperous businessmen, farmers, and professional men (not to mention well-known cricketers) are proud to retain – and to hear their children retain – their Yorkshire accents, whereas financial success and upward mobility among speakers of Cockney, Scouse, Brum, and broad Glaswegian are more often accompanied by rigorous attempts to modify their speakers' accents and, even more, those of their children.*

To recapitulate: the most stigmatized accents are those closely identified with the working classes in certain large industrial conurbations. The ability of such speakers to retain their accents and at the same time to be credited with the quality of educatedness is further limited by the range of speaking styles which have evolved among users of such accents. Nearly every language

---

* I recognize that this explanation does not cover the fact that other accents, like Tyneside's Geordie and the accents of industrial Lancashire, are also primarily associated with the lower classes, yet do not share this extreme disfavour. The reason for this remains a puzzle.

community in the world, however small and however limited its material culture, appears to recognize a quality which we we can call 'well-spokenness'. This is a form of speaking associated with such attributes as 'elegance and precision of utterance', and is especially called into play by the reading of poetry and by formal speech-making. Given the strong tradition of local dialect in certain regions of England, nobody doubts the ability of a speaker with a Yorkshire or Devon accent to give an impressive and acceptable rendering of a descriptive poem or a passage from the Bible. Speakers with the most stigmatized urban accents, however, appear to find it highly incongruous to adopt a formal or 'literary' speaking style while retaining the breadth of their accent. The more formal the words to be read, the greater the tendency to drop the characteristic features of their accent and approximate to the standard accent. The idea of the 23rd Psalm, the parable of the Good Samaritan, or Words-worth's 'Daffodils' being read with self-confidence and pride in a broad Cockney, Scouse, Birmingham or Glaswegian accent seems to contradict the canons of elegance, precision, and 'well-spokenness' generally.

The extension of educatedness, from being the property of a small elite, to something available to everyone who can take advantage of the mass education system, has thus not only helped elevate one accent – RP – to the highest prestige position, but has also helped devalue those accents which have the least perceived connection with literary forms of communication, which are esteemed more highly by the most educated people than are the more colloquial communication styles which form the basis of everyday living. These tendencies are not unique to Britain: in most countries of the world where a standard accent has developed in modern times, it is closely connected with percep-tions of educatedness and with the prestige given to a high level of literacy.

The United States has no real equivalent of RP, but the great majority of Americans for whom English is their mother tongue speak 'General American', which comprises that majority of accents which do not show strong eastern or southern characteristics, or features associated with the vernacular speech of Blacks or Hispanics. Regional differences of accent are far less important as a rule than differences associated with social class and education. Most New Yorkers, for example, can detect nonstandard features in the speech of their fellow-citizens and use these accent features as the basis of unfavourable judgements on such speakers. Like their counterparts in Britain, they do this even when their own speech is full of the accent forms they disparage in others. One US observer has claimed that nonstandard features in American English speech (grammar and vocabulary as well as accent) have the power to close off a conversation among strangers, bring job interviews to an abrupt end and, when used on the telephone, to render a flat advertised as vacant that morning suddenly to be declared "already let". Certainly there is the same general tendency in the United States for professional people to be expected to have divested their speech, in the course of extended education, of accent features associated with the working classes.

Another pointer to the critical role of educatedness in the way accents are judged is seen in Canada. Evaluation experiments among French-speaking Canadians in Quebec indicate that although the French Canadians who were studied claimed not to, in practice they showed an especially high regard for the model of spoken French represented by France itself, rather than the local (Canadian-French) norm. Here we clearly cannot be dealing with the influence of French economic or political power: the prestige which attaches to Parisian French is its perceived connection with educatedness and with the glories of the French literary culture to which a high level of education gives access.

Perhaps the most striking demonstration of the link between educatedness and accent in Britain was provided by a well-known experiment. Two comparable sixth-form groups in a secondary school were addressed by a male speaker, who was represented as a lecturer who had come to give a talk about the content of university psychology courses. The lecturer spoke RP and Brum equally fluently and used one accent with one group of pupils and the other with the second. A researcher then noted the pupils' reactions to each of the two performances. In his RP guise the lecturer was judged significantly more intelligent than as a Birmingham-accented speaker. He elicited considerably more co-operation from his audience and a much greater willingness to offer comments, especially favourable ones, on his suitability for this academic task. As many as half of those pupils who heard him with his RP accent made a point of commenting to the researcher on his well-spokenness, whereas the group who heard his 'Birmingham' performance tactfully refrained from mentioning any of his speech characteristics at all.

In this emerging pattern of associations with regional, social, and educational backgrounds which characterize our response to accents, there is one group that has been left out of our account. How do we react to non-British accents – to the accents of, for example, Americans or of those who have learned English as a foreign language?

The American accent – any American accent – can expect a favourable reception in Britain, for three reasons. First, its speaker is perceived as standing outside the social-class hierarchy which partly explains the scale of evaluation of our own British accents. Secondly, we are not able to judge, on accent alone, the features of 'educatedness' which might be apparent to native American listeners, so we give the speaker the benefit of the doubt. Thirdly, the American accent is to some extent glamorized by the film industry and by the number of American programmes shown on British television. Canadian English accents, which in Britain cannot normally be distinguished from American, share the same generally favourable evaluation. Australian, New Zealand, South African, and Indian accents will be examined in Chapter Six. Some, though not all, of these benefit, as do American accents, to an extent from their apparent classlessness, by which I mean that we cannot fit them into the class categories which are part of our scale of evaluation of British accents.

Our membership of the European Community means that we have frequent dealings with Germans, Frenchmen, and other fellow members (though less frequently with new members like the Portuguese and the Greeks). The accents of all these fellow-'Europeans' also benefit from standing outside easy classification in terms of social class, as many find when they come here to study, to work, and even to settle. An educated Englishman may feel able to marry a foreign girl from lower social-class origins because her accent does not advertise those origins, as it might well do if she had been brought up in this country. German and Austrian academics who sought refuge in Britain from Nazism after 1933 were remarkable for the extent to which they retained their strong German accents for forty years or more. Their ages at the time they fled were one factor; that their mother tongue was a language of educatedness in which they were still proud to think and converse even after their emigration also restrained their need to adapt to a very 'English' accent.

If RP has such enormous prestige, if other accents in Britain are less favoured than RP, and if a handful of accents associated with large industrial conurbations regularly involve their speakers in such adverse social reactions, and have done so for many years, it seems sensible to ask: *why doesn't everyone speak RP?*

A number of factors affect the extent to which differences of accent persist. As was seen in Chapter Two (and will be further discussed in Chapter Nine) the breadth of accents has declined since the mid-nineteenth century. Very few people now speak with the full-blown accents of the old dialects of that time; instead, the majority of working-class and lower-middle-class people are now midway between these historic forms and RP – in the area indicated on the accent diagram (page 54) as the mesolect. This movement towards RP is likely to continue, under the influence of education generally, of the mass media of the spoken word, and of the erosion of the traditional class system.

There are also limits to the ability of an individual to modify his accent, even if he or she decides to do so. Not everyone is aware of how he or she sounds. As one expert puts it, "Very many English people who have not heard their voices on tape imagine they have RP, whilst their neighbours have an 'accent'." Even when they have heard their own accent on tape, "the prestige of RP is so high that they are often unwilling to admit to themselves that they deviate from it." The ability to adapt readily to another accent seems to be related to age. Psychologists investigating the optimum age for learning to speak a foreign language without too much interference from one's native accent tend to agree that this ability declines markedly from the early teens onwards, though this is presumably also a function of each individual's ear for sound differences. The publishing tycoon Robert Maxwell, who came to Britain from Czechoslovakia when he was seventeen in the Second World War and whom most people would judge to speak English without any significant trace of a foreign accent, claimed in a BBC radio interview in 1987 that he learned to speak English within about six weeks of his arrival here. It is a matter of common observation that children can readily adopt a new accent in English at least until their teens, and many children up to that age maintain three separate accents, for home, for teachers, and for friends. Moving between accents already acquired is a form of what is called code-switching. Adapting one's accent (or acquiring a new one) beyond adolescence may easily lead to hyper-correction – when with one or two critical vowels, for instance, or with the attempt to avoid dropping *h*, the speaker takes the new accent to extremes and tends to sound phoney. A few individuals have the gift of mimicking a wide range of accents (and the particular voices of well-known figures who use them) and, as in the case of television's Mike Yarwood, this talent can he hugely entertaining. Some of the best anecdotes in our own and other cultures rely for their full effect on the deployment of a range of accents. Though some experts claim that accent flexibility has severely declined by the late teens, I know of many people who significantly modified their accents at university in their early twenties, and certainly people seem to be able to make small adjustments of accent even into old age.

So the powerful social pressures favouring adaptation to RP compete with factors limiting individuals' ability to do so, especially after adolescence. A further limitation on the general movement towards RP is the ambivalence about the system of values associated with this accent. If RP tends to be associated with educatedness and competence, non-standard accents gain their highest ratings as indicators of sociability and solidarity. To many people these values have been, and still are, more important than education or knowledge. Friendliness, co-operativeness and good-neighbourliness have all been crucial in the struggle for survival among working-class folk: privacy, keeping oneself to oneself, and the pursuit of personal ambition are luxuries which in the past were associated rather with the striving middle classes. The entire trade-union movement, which did so much to improve the lot of the working man and his family in the early years of this century, depended heavily on loyalty to the group. Never in recent years have accent – and indeed dialect – features been kept so prominently before the public eye and ear as in the ill-fated miners' strike of 1984–5, when day after day television programmes carried into every home in Britain the echoes of the Yorkshire miners' determination to defend "*us* pits and *us* jobs", with the 'us' pronounced like short *ooz*.

Nor is educatedness universally prized. Many people from humble backgrounds who have acquired it have described the obstacles they faced growing up in the sub-culture of the council estate or pit village, where to show an interest in serious reading was regarded as disloyal to the values of family and community. This was not true just of the grim world of the 1930s: it is reported during the 1940s and the 1960s and still goes on.

Given an individual's limitations in making major adjustments to his accent in later life, we can assert that an accent may tell us two things about a person: the part of the country in which he was born and the group with whose values he identifies himself. The fact that I have used the pronoun he/himself in its traditional sense of he/she, him/herself, underlines the need in this case to discriminate by gender, and to point out that women tend to be more adaptive towards the standard accent than men. Whatever the (probably complex) motivation for this, the benefits are striking, for research has shown that not only are women speakers of RP perceived as more competent than women with non-standard accents, but they are also thought to be less weak, and their ratings for adventurousness, independence and even femininity are all enhanced. By contrast, there is evidence that working-class males use non-standard accents and dialect features, especially during late adolescence and young manhood, as a badge of masculinity. Even while proclaiming their respect for 'correct' accent and grammar, they tend in practice to use local accent and grammatical features as an assertion of the 'roughness' and 'toughness' which are a dominant value in the macho sub-culture. Whether in the mouths of men or women, non-standard accents emphasize localism as against the values of the wider society. And teenagers have an additional motive to resist standard accents, as part of adolescent rebelliousness against adult values.

A fascinating piece of research by the American sociolinguist William Labov illustrates the tendency for accents to advertise different systems of values. Among the permanent residents of Martha's Vineyard, an island just off the coast of Massachusetts, Labov found that certain members of particular generations had developed specific accent features in order to assert their common identity in the face of the huge numbers of outside visitors who swamp them during the summer months, and to reassert their traditional values which were seen as threatened by the outsiders. The islanders themselves were barely aware of these accent differences, though in many other cases we know that changes of accent are made more deliberately.

Another interesting example comes from Wales. It is noticeable that many prominent supporters of the Welsh language are themselves speakers of RP. It has also been found that English-speaking adults in Wales who do not speak Welsh but are learning it have stronger Welsh accents in English than those who already speak Welsh. But any English-speaking Welshman is likely to adopt a Welsh accent in any conversation with an Englishman in which he feels that his Welsh identity is in some way under threat. Yet an 'ethnic' or 'national' identity is not always expressed by accent: sometimes a conflict of values occurs. Many educated Black people, both in the USA and Britain (as we see in Chapter Eight) when faced with a choice of expressing either their ethnicity or their educatedness in the way they speak, are willing to submerge their ethnic distinctiveness, in favour of speaking with the standard accent of the educated.

The idea that an accent can be perceived as embodying a set of attitudes and values provides us with what may be our most plausible explanation for the disfavour in which four or five accents associated with the uneducated citizens of grimy industrial conurbations are held. We still need to explore the reasons why rustic accents, by contrast with these – and by a reversal of the centuries-old disparagement of the countryman's speech – are so much more highly rated, so that the West Country accent may become the most significant asset of a politician, the Hampshire accent may be the essential ingredient in the public career of a famous cricket commentator, and the Chilterns accent, which the actor Bernard Miles frequently exploited, may have helped him on his way to a peerage. Several factors have contributed to the favourable reactions to rusticity. First, we remember that the British gentry and aristocracy before 1870 often grew up speaking, at least in childhood, with the accents of the regions in which their country estates were situated. Henry

Fielding in *Tom Jones* represents not only the eighteenth-century peasants as using local (southern) accent forms, but also Squire Western, who, when he gets worked up, occasionally lapses into it too, using words like *gu* for 'go', *vor* for 'for', and *zet* for 'set'. Interestingly, the womenfolk of his family never depart from standard English.

Secondly, relationships in the countryside between the lower classes and the gentry were to a considerable extent characterized by deference (though there were exceptions to this) and, as the Industrial Revolution progressed, it was the lower classes of the large industrial cities – so readily perceived as bearing the image of the mob – who offered a threat to the privileges of the established classes, while, as we have seen, the peasantry were a breed fast disappearing from the countryside by 1900. Finally, we need to note that strange phenomenon which invaded literature, painting, and many other aspects of British culture in the nineteenth century: an intense sentimentality about – almost a worship of – the countryside and all things rural. This may be our most important clue to the otherwise puzzling degree of glamour with which rustic accents continue to be associated in Britain.

FIVE

What is happening to RP?

The general picture which has emerged so far is illustrated by the diagram on page 54 which shows the relationship between the most non-standard accents (basilects), and the high-prestige standard accent (acrolect, represented by RP), with a wide area in between, represented by the graduations of accent between the two (mesolects). An especially posh form (marked RP), available to only a tiny minority of speakers, was identified (hyperlect), necessitating an extension leftwards and beyond mainstream RP. Indeed, few enough speak even the unmarked variety of RP – perhaps as few as three per cent of the population of Britain – but it has both high prestige and great power to influence the speakers of all the non-standard accents, and, especially if they have a high level of education, they will tend to move leftwards along the diagram and speak with an accent closer to RP. In general, education pulls in one direction only: it is difficult to set about learning a non-standard accent, especially one of the least favoured urban ones, because as soon as you ask their speakers to pronounce a certain word they are likely to give that word a sound which is closer to standard. Schoolteachers do not use the least favoured accent varieties, other than in a modified form, in teaching, though it is perfectly possible to learn an educated variety of a northern English accent, for example, by going to a school in the North of England. It is equally difficult to learn the hyperlect formally: it is spoken in only a tiny number of famous schools and Oxbridge colleges and there only by a minority of teachers and dons.

The first complication in this general picture has already been hinted at in examples given from Scotland and Wales. Outside England the acrolect becomes the hyperlect, so that people who imitate the unmarked RP of the BBC newsreader may in these regions be perceived an exhibiting the same kind of social pretension ('posh', 'affected', 'lah-di-dah', even *effeminate*) as greet the marked variety of RP from all those who do not themselves speak that hyperlect. This is truest of all in Australia, New Zealand, and South Africa, and for speakers of English in regions like West Africa and South-East Asia. It also applies to some extent within the British Isles, especially in any region where local models of educatedness have been establised, for example, Edinburgh Scottish, or the variety of Welsh English associated with schoolteachers, preachers, and a local intelligentsia.

There is a second complication which modifies that general picture in an important respect, and which will need to be marked by a new position on our diagram. Education, social ambition, and the example provided by the mass media of the spoken word, though steering large numbers of people in the direction of RP, achieve their maximum effect only with a certain proportion of those they influence. The accents of a very significant number of people who make this kind of transition stop fractionally short of 'pure' RP, retaining a few tiny traces of their original (say) Northern, or West-country vowels. To this category of 'almost-RP-but-not-quite' we can give the label PARALECT – the 'close-to' accent, whose closeness in this case is to the acrolect. Such speakers share much of the prestige of the acrolect (RP) and, even more, its associations with educatedness, but they retain just enough traces of the accent of their region of birth or upbringing to serve as a badge of their pride in those local origins. But notice that the retention of such tiny traces is much less likely to feature in the speech of educated people whose original accent was one of those four or five most disparaged ones, such as Cockney or Scouse.

Politicians like Denis Healey (who grew up in Bradford and graduated from Oxford) and distinguished BBC broadcasters like Brian Redhead (Newcastle-upon-Tyne, then Cambridge) show a very modified northern *a*; in Healey the vowel in *one*, *once*, and in the second syllable of *among*, and the vowel in the second syllable of *because*, retain their northernness. Healey's *s* in *because* has the soft northern quality rather than southern English's and RP's *z* sound. The final vowel in Redhead's *properly* makes the word come out more like *proplee*. The restoration of the value of the vowel sounds, as in the unstressed -ment in *development* or in the unstressed con- in *continue, condition*, is another of the small differences which keep the paralect of some northern speakers fractionally apart from RP. Russell Harty, who by the time of his early death in 1988 had become a successful TV interviewer and chat-show presenter, had entered Oxford from a school in the North of England. His pride in his northernness was obvious in his accent, yet his vowel sound in words like *but*, which in a typical northerner would rhyme with *soot*, in fact rhymed rather with *cert*, a sort of halfway compromise between northern and southern pronunciations. The number and nature of these often minute distinctions will make the difference between a close and a broad paralect. A broad paralect will shade into the infinite gradations of the mesolect, so that it becomes a moot point whether the accent of a well-known public figure like former Liberal party leader David Steel or of Neil Kinnock, the Labour party leader, is a broad paralect of some kind of mesolect, depending on how clearly the former's Scottishness or the latter's Welshness can be perceived from his accent. (What is certainly obvious is how close to RP many of David Steel's vowels have become.)Yet it is also true that the retention of only a very few non-RP features in a paralectal speaker's accent will cause that speaker's regional allegiance to be perceived. Brian Redhead is one of the ablest and most intellectually versatile performers in broadcasting today, and his rating for educatedness must be high on anyone's scale. Yet those minute northern traces in his accent still cause him to be seen as a northerner. Indeed, according to the writer of his profile in the *Sunday Times* in 1987, he is seen by friends, colleagues, and critics as "aggressively northern".

The simple accent diagram on page 54 now needs to be modified as follows:

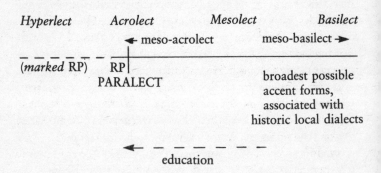

A powerful factor is now at work in British society which limits the leftward movement along this diagram of many educated and socially mobile people. This is the general erosion of class barriers and the consequently greater degree of democratization of Britain. Tendencies that have been at work since the end of the Second World War have come to a head in the period of the three Thatcher governments since 1979. Indeed, they help to explain Mrs Thatcher's resounding electoral successes in the face of high levels of unemployment. What we have seen for three decades or more is a decline in numbers of the manual working class and along with it a reduction in their 'collectivist' values and a reaching out towards middle-class values. In a 1972 survey 16 per cent of men of working-class origin considered themselves middle class; by 1986 the figure had risen to 23 per cent. Even if they do not necessarily regard themselves, in answers to opinion pollsters, as being middle class, many of them are enjoying a lifestyle formerly associated with the middle rather than the working classes, in terms of home-ownership, consumer goods, foreign holidays, and a higher degree of control over their incomes. Increased access to all of these for most people, especially those outside the category of the long-term unemployed, has greatly altered the perceptions and ambitions of the ordinary citizen. As the Labour MP Jack Straw commented in late 1987: "The working class is a dying and retreating group."

But democratization works both ways. Just as fewer people now regard themselves in any assertive sense as working class, so many people who were born to privilege or have achieved success through education and a career are made to feel that the old class distinctions that used to operate in their favour are socially divisive, and can now even be disadvantageous to them. This helps to explain the reluctance of the upwardly mobile to divest themselves of *all* traces of regional accents when moving very close to RP. It also explains the very limited distribution of the marked variety of RP. As we saw in Chapter Three, the enormous advantages of speaking the hyperlect up to the early part of the twentieth century outweighed the degree of ridicule which this accent often inspired among outsiders. The topmost segment of the British upper classes is, however, no longer cocooned in a world peopled exclusively by obsequious servants, by deferential tradesmen and by other 'toffs' like themselves. Its members have to acquire and hold down jobs – indeed, to compete for them. They have to work for, and with, other people from very different backgrounds. They have to get people to do things for them, often forms of service (like calling out a plumber in the middle of the night, or asking a similar 'favour' from a council employee) which are sought in circumstances in which the assertion of very high rank would be counter-productive: the imperious tone of marked RP has the distinct power to raise other people's hackles. The anthropologist Gerald Mars has studied cheating behaviour by various social and occupational groups, and described the 'fiddles' open to a dustman who charges householders for taking away unauthorized refuse. The sum charged relates to what the particular dustman thinks of the householder. "If someone says, 'Dustman' with a hoity toity voice, 'Will you take this away?' the dustman will say 'Oh I'm sorry, we can't take that, it's against the rules.' " Any British reader who, on moving house, finds that the removal men are managing to smash up his furniture, might like to try out (with an approximation to marked RP) the effect of the following sentence, whose three parts all represent the authentic idiom of the hyperlect: "I say, my good man, have a care!"

People still tolerate marked RP from members of the royal family, and indeed seem to expect it, though it is noticeable that while the Queen, the Queen Mother, and Prince Charles use elements of this accent, the Queen's younger sons, Prince Andrew and Prince Edward, do not: Andrew has unmarked RP and Edward's RP exhibits some of the more downmarket features which, as will be discussed, are creeping into modern RP. The Princess of Wales, who belongs to the same generation, is also said to have traces of these downmarket features. But outside the royal family and the grandest of the aristocracy, and perhaps outside the circles of the top civil servants and diplomats (especially older ones), and some members of the literary and artistic world and a few Oxbridge dons, the hyperlect is now more often seen as a handicap than an advantage.

Though leading public schools, whose pupils were experimenting with Cockney, Scouse and other varieties in the 1960s, have now reverted to the old mechanisms (like the shaming of new boys with very noticeable non-standard accents) which tend towards the production of RP, it is very much the unmarked rather than the marked variety – and for the very good reason that for many of the occupations such pupils would want to enter, a voice that was too posh would be a major disqualification. A personnel executive from the British branch of a multinational corporation which is a household name told me in 1984 that he now often receives applications from ex-public schoolboys who play down their educational origins, whereas a decade or two ago they would have made the most of them. Too privileged an education, or an accent which implies this, is felt to set limits on the extent to which one can get along easily with other people, a major requirement in most working situations.

The credibility which the unmarked RP accent gives its speakers, and the authority with which evaluation studies credit arguments expressed in it, may be an advantage in advertising and marketing, but, as we have seen, these advantages are not extended to the marked variety of RP. According to a student publication produced in Cambridge, public school products at that university nowadays became 'embarrassed and apologetic' about their backgrounds. Angela, a second-year undergraduate at Trinity College, is quoted as saying, "Eton accents are decidedly uncool – students from Eton wear ripped jumpers and torn jeans in an attempt to gain street-cred points. Once you get to Cambridge you'll discover that a comprehensive school background is 'hip'." This new emphasis on 'street-credibility' is itself a comment on the changing values of young people, at least during the transient student phase of their lives, if not later. At Oxford a *New Society* journalist investigating the background of a drugs scandal among upper-class undergraduates in 1986, wrote of the "mock Cockney accent" of some of his privileged informants, which nowadays "seems obligatory in Oxford".

The replacement of grammar schools by comprehensives, especially from 1965 onwards, meant that by 1986 some 90 per cent of the relevant age group within the state school system were enrolled in comprehensive rather than academically selective schools. One of the functions which many of the grammar schools used to set themselves was the promotion of RP, or, in some areas at least, the regional variety of 'well-spokenness'. Sometimes this was done crudely: a colleague once told me of his first day at a grammar school in the London area in the late

1930s when a teacher forcefully humiliated a fellow new boy for his non-standard vowels, making it frighteningly clear what kinds of adaptation were to be a condition of grammar school life. More often the promotion of the favoured accent was more subtle, and sometimes little more than a matter of teachers constituting models of educated speech for their pupils.

When schools became academically non-selective, the large proportion of less able pupils, who set little value on educatedness, made any emphasis on well-spokenness unrealistic, especially since the classroom subject 'English', which had often been the most obvious (though by no means the only) vehicle for the conscious teaching of pronunciation, was a prime target for the ideologically motivated passion for mixed-ability teaching groups. The aims of 'English' teaching from the 1960s onwards came, in many schools, to be dominated by a concern to explore and celebrate the child's *own* language in various forms of 'creative' self-expression. Training courses for future teachers of English reflected the widespread conviction of linguistic theorists that all languages, and all dialects of any one language, were 'equally good', and, in their own terms, equally 'correct'. For teachers to try to change children's speech by 'imposing' the grammar of standard English was held to be justifiable, if at all, only in terms of the demands of the examination system and of employers. Since spoken English was not normally tested in public examinations at ages sixteen or eighteen there was no justification at all on that score for trying to interfere with these accents. And even if they had wanted to discuss these issues sympathetically with their pupils, few classroom teachers of English would have had enough knowledge of linguistics or phonetics to know where to begin, since of the barely one in three classroom teachers of English who possessed *any* formal qualification in the subject, that qualification was overwhelmingly in English literature. Only a tiny handful of teachers of English beginning their careers in the 1960s and 1970s had any systematic training in English *language*.

Deficiencies in the specific knowledge of teachers of English combined with the egalitarian ideology which inspired the comprehensive school movement, to produce a deafening silence in schools on the subject. As was pointed out in Chapter One, the subject became, in the classroom, a taboo even more studiously avoided than sex – and even the taboo on sex was breaking down in the classrooms of the 1960s. In the midst of all these trends, a major beneficiary of the reorganization of schools on comprehensive lines was Britain's independent school system, which was given a new lease of life. One motive causing some parents to shun the new, non-selective schools was the fear of their children 'picking up an accent' (i.e. a less favoured variety) from their schoolfellows.

But if state school teachers are shy of discussing accents and in many cases hostile to the notion of trying to change the way their pupils speak, many of them continue to judge pupils by the way they speak and allow such judgements to affect their expectations of the academic potential of those pupils. Irrespective of their real ability – and sometimes in the face of contrary evidence from their written work – pupils whose accents show features of broad Cockney or of one of the varieties of West Indian English spoken in Britain may find that their teachers downgrade their expectations of their ability, and may even move them into a lower set or stream, or prepare them for a lower level of school-leaving examination. To the limited extent that teachers' expectations are self-fulfilling, the accents brought from home help some children to succeed in our educational system, and others to under-achieve.

Another area where 'democratization' has affected the prevalence of RP is the theatre. The psychologist Professor T. H. Pear reported attending a performance of *Hamlet* by an amateur dramatic society in a northern city in the early 1950s. Out of the twenty or so actors (all said to be northerners) only two had any identifiable northern features in their accent, and these amounted to less than one in a thousand sounds. Until the 1960s part of the training of professional actors and actresses involved equipping them to speak with the RP accent, but it is now common for older members of the theatrical community – and critics like the author Anthony Burgess – to deplore the fact that the most famous drama schools have in recent decades made no attempt whatsoever to provide their students with facility in RP or indeed any disposition to want to be able to speak it.

When the future playwright Joe Orton decided in 1950 to train as an actor, he resolved to lose every vestige of his working-class origins and poor education, and took private elocution lessons to eradicate his Leicester accent. So successful was he that he later came top in a diction test at the Royal Academy of Dramatic Art – in the days when drama schools still rewarded this kind of 'well-spokenness'. When the actor Leo McKern (star of the successful TV series *Rumpole of the Bailey*) came to England from Australia in 1947, he worked hard to lose his Australian accent. The widely acclaimed television actor Leonard Rossiter, who died in his fifties in 1984, grew up in humble circumstances in Liverpool. Without the benefit of attendance at drama school, virtually his only formal theatrical training was the elocution lessons he took to rid himself of the Liverpool accent which would seriously have limited his repertoire.

Bill Fraser, famous as Judge Bullingham in that same *Rumpole* series, and even more so as TV's Sergeant-Major Snudge (to Alfie Bass's Bootsie) and successful in a number of serious stage roles, was a Scot who left his native Perth as a young man to make his way on the stage in London. Living in great poverty and often sleeping rough, he set himself the task of "learning English", which involved reciting for hours sentences like, "While I was on the balcony eating salmon I saw a mass of people on the grass." The actor George Cole left school, and his south London home, aged fourteen to join a musical on tour as an understudy. He gives credit for his successful career to the older actor Alistair Sim, who with his wife made Cole his protégé and "did a Professor Higgins job" on Cole's stark Tooting accent. Sim's own early career had been as an elocutionist giving speech-training lessons to Scottish Presbyterian ministers. The ability to switch on authentic traces of his Tooting vernacular is an essential element of George Cole's success as the character Arthur ('Arfur') Daley in the long-running TV series *Minder*, but he could never have sustained a career as an actor on stage and television if he had been limited to this one, non-standard, variety of accent.

The general movement in recent decades towards greater social equality and an accompanying 'democratization' of speech forms (of which one trivial manifestation is the popularity in London of 'squire' in place of the too deferential 'Sir' and the too familiar 'mate') have led to changes in the nature of RP itself. First, there has been a reaction away from any trace of the features which, when they predominate, constitute marked RP. Several of the best-known BBC newsreaders who started their careers in the 1930s had accents which, while not identifying them as speakers of the ducal hyperlect, nevertheless exhibited traces of these vowels. This was true of John Snagge and also of Stuart Hibbert – the latter had *awf, crawss* and *lawst*. When the BBC began its television service in the 1930s, one of the first two woman presenters chosen had slight traces of marked RP (she also had aristocratic connections): the other had a very strong marked RP accent. On cinema newsreels of that period and indeed throughout the war, the narrators often used more of the marked RP features than would be used by a BBC or TV narrator today, and the same was true of documentaries and instructional films. The automatic warning announcements in lifts at some London underground stations give the impression of having been recorded in that earlier period, to judge from the quality of the vowels in the three key words of the message "Stand clear of the gates!" As late as the early 1950s the dialogue of middle-class characters in the genre of British-made films known as 'Ealing comedies' was spattered with the sounds of *awf, clawth,* and other marked RP words. It would be an instructive linguistic exercise to identify systematically the changes in the accents used by Celia Johnson and Trevor Howard in the famous 1945 film *Brief Encounter* and in the television film *Staying On* (1980). In the earlier film their performances were characterized not only by strong traces of marked RP, but also by the clipped variety of speech so well exemplified by actors of the Noël Coward era.

The second source of change in the nature of RP is the 'popular' speech of London. In Chapter Two, great emphasis was laid upon the disproportionate influence of London in the cultural evolution of the nation and especially of its speech forms, particularly since the fifteenth and sixteenth centuries. In this instance it is not the speech of highly educated and sophisticated groups centred on London, such as gave birth to mainstream RP, nor the aristocratic circles who developed the exclusive hyperlect, but rather the speech of the 'man and woman in the street' that is influential. The label *Cockney* suggests a really broad variety associated with the least educated, and containing a regularized set of vowel variations from RP, plus systematic *h*-dropping: *fin* for 'thin', *bovver* for 'bother', *marf* for 'mouth', an extra vowel in *loverly* (lovely), also in *Enery* and *umberella*; *toon* and *dook* (for 'tune' and 'duke', as in most forms of American English), and a whole proliferation of rhyming slang which since the early nineteenth century has popularized such forms as *trouble and strife* (wife), *plates of meat* (feet) *mince pies* (eyes) and a few which have passed into standard English, as in 'use your loaf' (loaf of bread = head). Originally associated with the innermost areas of east London adjacent to the sound of Bow Bells, this Cockney dialect has spread out among working-class neighbourhoods in a sprawling metropolis on both sides of the Thames. But the speech of the majority of lower-class Londoners certainly does not exhibit the full range of these features. It is, in fact, a mesolect (see the diagram on page 82) in many ways considerably closer to RP.

The distinguished phonetics expert, Dr John Wells of University College, London, calls this the 'popular' London accent.

'Popular' London speech is today the greatest single influence not only on RP itself but also on the accents of many other parts of Britain. Overspill from the huge metropolitan conurbation of London has carried families who speak with the 'popular' London accent to live out in English country towns as distant as Basildon, Peterborough, Basingstoke, and Andover. As the centre of production and distribution for a number of industries, activities, and communications media which exercise a formative influence on popular taste, London sets fashions which are imitated the length and breadth of the land, and indeed throughout the world.

This 'popular' London accent threatens the 'purity' of several RP vowels; more importantly, it has given RP two major features discernible in the accents of prominent and high-prestige RP speakers as well as masses of less exalted folk whose speech shows no obvious sign of regional or lower-class origin. The first is what is technically called '*t*-glottalling'. In the sentence:

"There's a lot of it about"

the *t*s at the end of *lot*, *it* and *about* are 'strangled' so as to produce:

"there's a lo' of i' abou'."

This feature, which is long established in 'popular' London speech, is now commonly heard among RP speakers in the South of England. Prince Edward has at least a trace of it, as in his question to reporters about a charity performance:

"What did you think of i'?"

where i' stands for *it*. Phonetics experts have also claimed to detect it in the speech of the Princess of Wales, a claim which prompts two comments. First, it is entirely to be expected that a young lady of her background, her generation (she is twelve years younger than Prince Charles), and with her previous experience of living, working and flat-sharing in London, should exhibit such a feature. Secondly, it is presumably only a matter of time before her speech becomes the 'Queen's English' (even if only that of the Queen consort) and to that extent influential – at least in theory. In any case, the Princess of Wales's immense popularity, the media interest she generates, and her position as a leader of fashion, all guarantee that many things she does and says will be treated by some people as a model. The fact that the Duchess of York also has traces of this feature in her speech is confirmation of its influence.

When the BBC Radio 1 disc jockey and raconteur, Simon Bates, recently said on his regular programme:

"They get on better now than they've ever gone before"

his millions of (mostly young) listeners could presumably interpret more easily than I was able to, his 'gone' as *go(t) on*. Recently I tutored a French student who was teaching in a comprehensive school in Cambridgeshire while completing her English studies for a degree in a French university. I was puzzled by the consistency with which she glottallized ('strangled') the *t*s at the ends of most of her words. It transpired that the town in which she lived and taught had a large proportion of overspill Londoners in its population. This, and the speech of some of the younger RP-speaking staff members, were presumably the cause. (It had, of course, nothing to do with the fact that the French do not pronounce the *t*s at the end of many words in their own language.) Cockney extends this treatment of the *t* sounds at the ends of words, to *t* sounds in the middle of words, and so also, for example, does Glaswegian, so that

"a better bit of butter"

loses not only the *t* of *bit* but also the *tt* of *better* and of *butter*. (Whereas Cockney follows RP in not having an *r* sound at the end of those two words, Glaswegian has a very strong *r* in both.) However, so far, the tendency for RP to incorporate '*t*-glottalling' for the *t*s at the *end* of words has not extended to the *t*s in the *middle* of words, which remains a highly stigmatized feature of both Cockney and Glaswegian.

The other major influence of 'popular' London speech on present-day RP is heard in the tendency for the sound *l* in certain words to be turned into something more like *w*, as happens in words like *milk*. This is a traditional London sound, making St *Paul's* come out like St *Paw's*, and *parcel* like *par-saw*. Dr John Wells reports being told by a man from the East End of London, called Walter, that until he learned to read and write he had always thought his name was *Water*. Traces of this tendency are observable in modern RP, though it is not yet as widely noticeable as the glottalling of *t* at the ends of words.

My final example of the way RP has been moving downmarket in recent years by incorporating previously stigmatized features from 'popular' London speech is the single word *garage*. About twenty years ago there was a fairly clear distinction between three pronunciations of garage. Although they did not conform exactly to the distinctions between hyperlect (marked RP), acrolect (unmarked RP), and mesolect (majority of non-standard accents), they reflected very much the same kinds of division; they also tended to fit the division into upper, middle and lower class, with 'educatedness' ascribed to 1 and 2, but not 3:

1. GaRAGE: stress on the second syllable, which was pronounced as in French, and as in English words borrowed from French like *mirage* and *camouflage*.

2. GArage: same pronunciation as 1, but with the stress brought forward on to the first syllable.

3. GArage: stress on the first syllable, but the second syllable pronounced to rhyme with *marriage*.

Round about 1980 the least prestigious form (3) began to come into common use in mainstream RP, being heard quite commonly – here's a useful test for the acceptability of any pronunciation – from BBC and ITV newsreaders (of national rather than local news programmes).

Though I have claimed that democratization and greater equality have in recent years made the marked variety of RP more of a liability than an advantage for most purposes, and caused mainstream RP to move downmarket by taking on some features which twenty years ago were unacceptable to RP speakers, there are limits to this general tendency, at least at present. Certainly a whole range of non-standard features, particularly some associated with lower-class accents, remain 'beyond the pale' and their use can instantly deny the speaker any assumption of educatedness. The *-in* for *-ing* suffix has almost completely disappeared from the speech of the aristocracy who once (as we saw) went huntin' and shootin', and its survival in a large number of non-standard accents is still heavily stigmatized. *H*-dropping, for which the aristocracy developed a clever system which differed from that of the lower classes, survives in a very limited number of contexts among speakers of the hyperlect, including some members of the royal family. Ours is not the only language and culture in which *h*-dropping among the common people is stigmatized: we are told that Galilean speakers of Aramaic in New Testament times were well known for this tendency, so that Jesus Christ almost certainly dropped his *h*s. It was thus not inappropriate that a BBC Schools Radio programme on the life of Christ in September 1985 should have endowed him with a Yorkshire accent, since Yorkshire folk are among those whose accent permits *h*-dropping, as do all the urban accents of England (especially Cockney, as Dickens constantly reminds us) except the Geordie accent of Tyneside. The accents of Scottish and Irish English tend not to drop *h*s, and the same is true of the Americans, though some Australians do.

Few would disagree with Dr John Wells's comment that the way a speaker uses the aspirate (i.e. *h*) at the beginning of a word appears to be "the single most powerful pronunciation shibboleth in England". He reports the remark of a London schoolteacher that he only has to look sternly at any child who drops an *h*, and that child will say the word again, "this time correctly". Among the few *h*-droppers to leap the barriers raised around this accent feature in modern times have been Cabinet ministers who came from trade-union backgrounds, like J. H. Thomas, the railwaymen's leader who became Colonial Secretary in the National Government in the 1930s, and George Tomlinson, who in Attlee's great reforming government of 1945–50 became Minister of Education – an area especially sensitive to outward and audible criteria of educatedness. Above all, there was Ernest Bevin, who rose from a background of poverty and illegitimacy to become from 1945 to 1951 a great Foreign Secretary with ultimate responsibility for the diplomatic service, the repository in that period of some of the most conservative forms of accent snobbery. Bevin, whose schooling was sketchy in the extreme, and who became a delivery boy by the time he was thirteen, retained his broad Somerset accent and non-standard grammar throughout his exalted political career. It was reported that once during a Cabinet meeting he said something that sounded like, "That can be left to you and I, Prime Minister." Nobody could be quite sure whether he was saying *you and I* (you and me); *Hugh and Nye* (Hugh Gaitskell and Aneurin – ('Nye') – Bevan); *Hugh and I*; or *you and Nye*. His accent did not discriminate among these four possibilities.

Of all these political figures, none dropped his *h*s with a greater flourish than 'Jimmy' Thomas. *Hansard* reporters could never be sure if he was referring to the *Highlands* or *islands* of Scotland. An MP from 1910 onwards, he was an affable man who made friends in all parties, including F. E. Smith, the future Conservative Lord Chancellor, who had some reputation as a wit. One story tells how Thomas was complaining to a group of MPs after a gruelling day in the Commons, "I've got a 'ell of a 'eadache!" F. E. Smith's reply was instantaneous: "What you want, Jim, is a couple of *aspirates*."

SIX

Accent variety and the mass media

When we hear, especially for the first time, a speaker of English who uses an accent other than our own, our reaction to what that speaker says is influenced by three main factors:

1. intelligibility;
2. distraction; and
3. prejudice.

First, the words may be pronounced in an accent so different from any we are used to hearing that the actual meaning of what is said is unintelligible. Secondly, though we may understand the words, our attention is distracted from the message by our preoccupation with the fact that this is a relatively unfamiliar set of sounds. Thirdly, the whole set of stereotyped evaluations which we examined in Chapter Four may come into play. If we are English, we are likely to rate the speaker more highly on a number of positive qualities if he uses a standard accent, less highly if he uses one of a certain group of non-standard ones, and generally very unfavourably if it is one of the four or five most disfavoured ones.

In Britain, not to have a *colour* TV set has almost become an index of living on the poverty line. It has been estimated that the average British family watches television for twenty-two hours a week – some surveys suggest even more – and in the case of adults living alone, or children during the school holidays, this figure increases to thirty-six hours a week. In many homes a number of radios spread around different rooms – and now, increasingly, additional TV sets also – entertain different members of the household. Most cars have radios fitted as standard, and for many people this is their main opportunity for extended listening to radio programmes, apart from the early morning when breakfast radio still has a large audience. In advanced countries of the world cinema-going has declined (though video-viewing has burgeoned), while among the developing nations films still attract huge audiences.

This massive use of radio, television, film, and video vastly increases the amount of exposure to the sound of the human voice in its many guises, and hence the number of occasions when listener reactions to the factors of intelligibility, distraction, and prejudice are likely to operate. In this chapter I examine some of the consequences of this, and look especially at the ways in which our perceptions of certain national or regional groups are influenced by the way their accents are used by the mass media of the spoken word as well as in our everyday dealings with them.

If the greatest single influence on the current evolution of English RP and of many non-standard accents in Britain today is the 'popular' London accent, it is also true that the greatest single influence on the grammar, vocabulary, and idiom of English as spoken and written in Britain is American English. This is because of the substantial number of American-made films and serials shown on Britain's four TV channels, and because of the influence, especially on writers and journalists, of books, magazines, and other written material originating in the USA. American idiomatic usages such as 'do have' for 'have got' have invaded British English, and I have watched the development in my own TV-addicted children of US grammatical forms such as the simple past rather than the perfect tense with the adverbs *yet*, *just*, or *already*, expressing time ('I already did it' for 'I have already done it').

In the speech and writing of respected colleagues, 'overly' has replaced our own 'excessively', and 'off limits' now competes with 'out of bounds'. Words newly coined in the USA cross the Atlantic in hundreds every year to enrich our vocabulary, sometimes hustling out perfectly good and long-established words carrying the same meaning. This influence is a one-way process, a reward for all we did to establish their language and culture before 1776. They expect – and get – virtually nothing by way of linguistic innovation in return. But all this exposure to American voices on our television screens has little impression on our various British *accents*. There are a few words, like *harass*, in which the American stress pattern (in this case on the second syllable) now seems to be taking over in RP (which up till now had it on the first), but that US pronunciation was already current anyway in some British regional accents.*

In Chapter One the convenient term 'General American' was used for the most widely used form of American accent which has no noticeable regional characteristics. An alternative term is Network English, referring to the type of accent most acceptable to the US TV network, a connection which reminds us of the important role of the mass media of the spoken word in standardizing an accent across local boundaries within a nation.

There are a small number of fairly regular differences between the standard form of American accent and RP. All the sounds of American English exist in RP, even if we do not use them in exactly the same way. Americans pronounce a strong *r* in *card, port*, and similar contexts, which RP had lost by 1800 but which is also present in, for example, Scots and Irish accents, in many Lancashire varieties, and in 'West Country'. Americans have a 'short' *a* in *dance* and *path* where RP has a longer one, but most northern English accents share the American form. Americans

---

* In a BBC Radio 4 programme in 1982 on sexual harassment, the presenters began by stressing the first syllable of *harass* and *harassment*; half the interviewees on the programme stressed the second syllable, and by the end of the programme one of the presenters had moved the stress to the second.

do funny things with the vowel represented by *o*, which causes words like *hot* to sound like RP's *heart*, and make *bother* rhyme with *father*. Some American speakers make this even more complicated for British listeners by giving a completely different treatment to the *o* in *dog*, so that *hot dog* sounds to us rather like 'heart dawg'. In a press item dictated by telephone from the United States to *The Times* in London in the 1960s by a journalist with an American accent, the word *gods* appeared throughout the article as *guards* – to the great mystification of the readers next day – because it had been taken down by an RP speaker at this end.

The fact that many Americans do not distinguish between the sounds of *marry*, *Mary*, and *merry* causes British listeners little problem, since the meaning of those words is normally made clear by the different contexts in which they are used. It is simply not true to claim, as one British academic has done, that Americans are "a people unable to distinguish between their donkeys and their buttocks" on the grounds that our pronunciation (and spelling) make a distinction between *ass* and *arse*, where Americans have 'ass' for both. Such a claim is the equivalent of saying that it is impossible in English to distinguish between a young attendant and the side of a leaf of paper, since both have a word with the same sound (page).

American English removes the *y-* from the *yu-* sound when it turns *new* and *duke* into *noo* and *dook*, but, as has been mentioned, so do some British regional accents, for example in the south and east. For good measure Americans insert this full *yu-* sound at the front of the second syllable of *figure*, which, at least in England, we do not.

Distraction rather than unintelligibility is likely to affect the British reaction to the US pronunciation of many foreign words, especially proper names. The short *oo* (as in *good*) of the first syllable of RP's *Buddha* and *Buddhist* compares with the American longer *oo* as in *boot*, and they have *cow* for the British *co* in *Moscow*. Americans pronounce Nepal *nay-pahl* and rhyme the second syllable of *Vietnam* with RP's *palm* where we rhyme it with *dam*, but a reverse process operates for the way Englishmen and Americans treat the *a*s in both syllables of *Pakistan*, though the Scottish pronunciation of the word is similar to the American.

Much the greatest cause of difficulty for Britons in understanding the American accent is the treatment of *t*, which in many contexts Americans produce as a sound like *d*, or even drop altogether. Context often fails to clarify whether the American speaker means *riding* or *writing*, *meddle* or *metal*, *deluded* or *diluted*, the *war dead* or the *war debt*, or – a crucial distinction – *inter-city* or *inner-city*. The worst example of all is *can't*. RP uses a different vowel sound in *can't* from *can*; Scottish accents which do not make this distinction tend to be meticulous about pronouncing the *t*. Some accents, like Geordie and the adjacent Wearside, remove all possibility of doubt by using the full-blown *cannot* (but with a stress pattern similar to *carrot*). Yet Britons get the impression that large numbers of Americans go through their whole lives unable to make a confident distinction between a positive and a negative statement of possibility, between 'I can do it' and 'I can't do it.'

Nevertheless, in general it is true that people in Britain develop an extensive *passive* knowledge of American-spoken English. The converse seems not always to be true. A writer in a British educational journal in 1985 wrote from Washington of having just met an American who told him proudly that he could receive both BBC1 and BBC2 television channels by virtue of his satellite dish. "But I never watch them," he added. "I can't understand a word they say." However, this cannot be typical. It is true that there has been prejudice across the Atlantic against the marked RP accent that was once common on the lips of high-ranking British officials there, and it was claimed that the 'sissy' accents of British spokesmen sent over before Pearl Harbor to gain support for Britain's war effort were counterproductive to their case. But some recent reports from the USA suggest that Americans now get so much exposure to British accents on their media that they no longer think them strange. Indeed, in certain contexts a British (RP) accent is regarded as having high prestige – for example, on the stage. An American accent is seen as less appropriate than a British (RP) one to the portrayal of Shakespeare's characters and those of the other great classics of the theatre repertory. This evaluation does not, however, necessarily extend to British regional accents.

An American finance company planning to build its European headquarters in Britain was reported in 1986 as having ruled out three potential sites in Wales (Cardiff, Newport, and Clwyd) because of the "grating and irritating" local accents. Its spokesman elaborated: "The lilting Welsh accent is a total turn-off sales-wise." He referred to three independent surveys which, he claimed, had all shown the Welsh accent to be "the most unacceptable for British marketing". If such surveys actually existed, it would be interesting to know how many British accents were included, since this judgement on Welsh accents is not in line with the evaluations of British hearers generally, though admittedly these were not tested on behalf of a credit card firm. Perhaps the 'Taffy' stereotype of the Welshman still has powers to influence some people's reactions.

Australian accents pose few problems of intelligibility in Britain, and their 'distraction' effect is rapidly being reduced by their increasing familiarity to viewers of British television. Just over a hundred years ago, the first thing to strike an English academic visiting Australia was, he later claimed, "the pure English that was spoken there". But this opinion of Australian spoken English has not been shared by the majority of Britons since that time; indeed the Cockney origins and associations of the Australian accent have more often been a matter for adverse comment. As there is hardly any regional variation among Australian accents, the main distinction is between 'broad Australian', 'general Australian' and 'educated (or 'cultivated') Australian'. In fact it was only relatively recently that Australians with the highest degree of education began to show a real pride in having any Australian accent at all.

The Australian author and social critic Donald Horne describes in his autobiography how as a student at Sydney University around 1939 he made efforts to change his accent because "it seemed a negation of education to speak like an Australian". To change involved practising RP vowels with the help of a phonetics textbook. The breakthrough came with the emergence of a home-grown educated class of sufficient numbers, when native-born Australians outnumbered Englishmen and other incomers as university professors, judges, Anglican arch-bishops, and headmasters of the most prestigious independent schools. Even so, any breadth of Australian accent was normally regarded as unacceptable in the thriving Australian film industry which grew up in the 1960s and 70s, and this attitude was reflected in the accents of actors, announcers, and presenters on Australian television for two decades until the mid-1970s, so that viewers heard more American accents and close Australian paralects of RP than 'real' Australian accents, even in television commercials. Two of the best-known Australians in Britain are writers and TV personalities Clive James and Germaine Greer, in both of whose speech the influence of RP is now pre-dominant.

Back home, the Australian Labour Prime Minister Bob Hawke exemplifies the opposite process. Having built his political career on the power-base of the trade-union movement, he has, despite his privileged education at the universities of Western Australia and Oxford, sought to emphasize, by the breadth of his Austra-lian accent, his identification with the common man. This was symbolized by the words of acknowledgement for the support of his wife, Hazel, which he spoke as he celebrated his third successive general election victory in July 1987 – "Hizel's a grite mite." Several of his colleagues in the Labour government, however, who come from much humbler and less educated backgrounds, have made the opposite transition and toned down the broadness of their Australian accents.

By the mid-1980s it had become possible for British television viewers to follow three different Australian soap operas a day on most days of the week. Their popularity relates to credible acting, interesting story lines, and the general attractiveness to the British of the Australian lifestyle, especially the relative class-lessness of Australian society. Such programmes, combined with other Australian material on British television, and the generally high quality of Australia's modern film industry, have accus-tomed the British to the moderate and often slight degree of Australian accent which actors tend to use, and to earn that form of accent a new respect. The broadest Australian accents, however, are still regarded (as they tend also to be in Australia) as unlikely to indicate educatedness in a speaker,* and it is in conformity with the older stereotype of the anti-intellectual, coarse, macho, beer-swilling Australian of the outback that *broad* Australian accents – along with hints of unprintable exple-tives – are used on British TV commercials to promote the sales of beer. This example was singled out in a letter to the *Sunday Times* in December 1986 in a correspondence concerning adver-tisements which cause revulsion against the product advertised. The writer claimed that it "put me right off Australia and all things Australian".

After the American and Australian accents, the variety of non-British accent which impinges most upon listeners in Britain is Indian English. This, as we saw in Chapter One, is a generalized term for the accents of the many regions of the different states of the Indian subcontinent (Pakistan, India, Bangladesh, Sri Lanka, and Nepal), most of which, however, exhibit a great

---

* Whether any breadth of Australian accent is compatible with, say, a performance of Shakespeare, is still in doubt. Anthony Holden, biographer of Prince Charles, experienced it in 1981 at a production of *Hamlet* at Sydney Opera House ("symbol of Australia's cultural renaissance"). "Aware of my Pom prejudice, I have to leave: 'to buy or not to buy', I just can't."

number of common characteristics which have grown up since the English language was established in the nineteenth century as the official language of education, but taught largely by indigenous teachers. India is the third largest publisher of books in the English language, though there may be barely 30 million in the whole subcontinent who are literate in English. India is also a major exporter of graduates, and in western Europe, Africa, the Gulf States, and North America it is not unusual to come across doctors and dentists, teachers in schools, polytechnics and universities, and other professionals, who have originated from the subcontinent. From the 1960s there has been a strong flow of immigration into Britain from India (and of Indians from East Africa, especially following Idi Amin's expulsion of Asians in 1972) and more recently also from Bangladesh. Whole areas of certain cities have been settled by such Asians, many of whom bring skills, entrepreneurship, and habits of hard work and personal courtesy which have helped transform the quality of life in some previously blighted neighbourhoods.

Indian English accents are little heard on British radio and television. They are more likely to be encountered in a consultation with a doctor or dentist, in a lecture or class in a school or college, or in a similar professional context. British Rail and other transport systems employ numbers of such speakers on their staffs and it is common to hear such accents in use in announcements on railway public-address systems or occasionally in arguments involving ticket inspectors.

"There are Indians with a fair knowledge of English whose accent is so impenetrable that English people can only understand them, if at all, with the greatest difficulty," writes London University's leading expert in phonetics, Dr John Wells. After winning the Booker Prize in 1981 for *Midnight's Children*, the novelist Salman Rushdie – born in India but educated at Rugby School and Cambridge – revisited India with his (English) wife, and the trip was made the subject of a BBC television documentary. In it Rushdie recounted how his wife had had a conversation on a train with an Indian intellectual: each thought the other was speaking a different language.

The vowel system of the Indian English of more educated speakers is not widely different from the RP from which it is ultimately derived. Some consonants create difficulty. The state television service in India uses newsreaders who approximate, to a greater or lesser degree, to RP. On an academic visit to India in September 1986 I was slightly surprised to hear a reference in a TV news bulletin to "the wise president", which seemed to me to be taking deference to the point of sycophancy. It was a moment or two before I realized that the dignitary concerned was the vice-president: *w* and *v* are often not distinguished from each other in Indian English, and *s* and *z* are also interchanged in some contexts, or omitted altogether, as in plural endings (e.g. 'the work' for the work*s*) and third person singular forms of present-tense verbs (e.g. 'he work' for he work*s*).

By far the greatest source of unintelligibility in the Indian English accent is its pattern of word stress – that is, deciding which syllable in a word gets the emphasis. Despite all the differences between RP and the other accents of Britain, in the sounds of vowels and of a few consonants, despite the *h* dropping rules and *-in* and *-ing* endings, all words spoken, with negligible exceptions, share the same stress pattern. Often the placing of stress on one syllable rather than another alters the meaning: compare to perMIT (verb) with a PERmit (noun). The American accent sounds noticeably different from RP, yet apart from a handful of words like deTAIL, baTON, INquiry, LABoratory, adverTISEment – and harASS whose stress pattern we have seen invading RP, as REsearch has already done – the Americans put the stress on the same syllable of the word as the British do. The same is true of Australian, New Zealand, and South African accents, and largely true of West Indian accents, though not of West and East African varieties.

Indian English, however, has revolutionized the established stress pattern of English as spoken throughout most of the world.

Thus reGRET becomes REGret, deVELop becomes DEVelop, and we hear DESTroy, ARRested, neCESSary, PREPare, DEFence, REFer, and a thousand more. Indian academics lecture to international audiences on important (sometimes IMportant) EVents (or E-*w*ents), and Indian specialists in economics who have lectured for years in British and American universities go on calling their subjects eCONomics. One Indian researcher has estimated that in as many as *one in five* of all the words in Indian English the word stress is put on a different syllable from that used in RP and the rest of the English-speaking world. Furthermore, this proportion of one-fifth of the total word-stock is made up mostly of 'content' words which carry most of the meaning of the sentence, rather than 'connecting' words which are often less crucial – though Indian English even manages to achieve a different stress pattern in a humble preposition like *towards*, making it rhyme with *cowards*.

Failure to acknowledge the extent to which Indian English differs from British English and most other varieties of English in the world has led to a high degree of misunderstanding. In many instances this is potentially dangerous in, for example, consultations between patient and doctor, where the patient speaks British English and the doctor Indian English, or vice versa. In the 1960s and 70s Britain's National Health Service relied heavily on the services of doctors from the Indian subcontinent, especially for hospital posts, but problems of intelligibility were one of the factors which led to the institution of an examination in English language use as well as in medical competence to be taken before overseas doctors are allowed to practise in Britain. In 1980 the pass rate was 43 per cent, in 1985 22 per cent; of 757 doctors qualifying in India only 195 got through. In 1986 there were 1,876 candidates for the examination, the majority from the subcontinent: 77 per cent failed. Many Indian graduates appointed to teach in British schools in the past three decades have faced similar problems of intelligibility, and other occupations where communication is important have also been vulnerable. In America, a federal judge declared in 1982 that the State of Washington had the right to bar a Pakistan-born employee from a job as an auditor because his heavily accented English made him hard to understand.

Using speakers of Indian English to make public announcements at stations or on trains leads to similar difficulties. During the exceptionally severe winter of January 1987, when parts of the country were snowbound, a guard's announcement to passengers on an Intercity 125 train from the Midlands to London's St Pancras was prefaced by a reference in which *intercity* was given a stress pattern that rhymed it with *university*, and the content of the message itself, intended to give some crucial information about which rail services were operating on an emergency basis and which ones had been cancelled, was completely unintelligible to the great majority of the passengers.

These problems result from the taboo against the discussion of accents and their relative intelligibility. If a speaker of heavily accented Indian English were refused employment as a guard because of the likelihood of his having to make public announcements whose intelligibility in an emergency would be of vital significance, there would be an immediate accusation of racism. In fact, the use of a speaker with a broad Glaswegian accent would produce a similar incomprehension, though in this instance because of his vowels and consonants (and especially his glottal stop) rather than his pattern of word stress.

The problems associated with understanding Indian English in Britain are, however, transient: we are dealing here with an age-group of immigrants who, within a couple of decades, will have retired from the jobs in which their speech forms are a barrier to communication. Their sons and daughters, born in Britain (as is the case now with more than half of Britain's Asian population), tend to speak with the accents of the locality in which they have grown up. Those who experience extended education will tend to speak RP or a paralect whose word-stress pattern follows the international rather than the Indian English model. In India itself, the children of the wealthy who have attended boarding schools modelled on the English public school often speak RP with traces of the hyperlect, and with some of the schoolboy slang of British prep schools and public schools – and school stories – of fifty years ago or more, and perhaps with the regimental slang of the same period. Rajiv Gandhi, who went to such a privileged school in India, and afterwards to Cambridge, has an accent and word-stress pattern far closer to RP than to Indian English.

Since English as spoken in West Africa has a similar problem affecting word stress, the large number of students in Britain from that region, and particularly from Nigeria, will continue to encounter problems in making themselves understood.

Another variety of accent in English with which people in Britain are frequently confronted which has an idiosyncratic word-stress pattern is English as spoken by the French. If they stressed the same syllables as in Indian English it might be a help, but French speakers of English have a word-stress pattern all their own, which contributes more to their unintelligibility than do the predictable overlay of French vowels or such features as the French difficulty with the English *h-*. The late Peter Sellers was well known for his representation, popularized by films and records, of the accent of an Indian doctor and of the mangled vowels of his French detective, Inspector Clouseau. Credible as he was in both guises, even he did not do anything like justice to the differences in word stress which characterize speakers of Indian English, and most Frenchmen when they speak English.

Even those French speakers who have gone to some trouble to achieve a high standard of spoken English are apt to betray themselves by such gallicisms. Around 1980 a senior French political figure was made the subject of a BBC radio profile. The programme was the more interesting because of the politician's admirable fluency in English. Listeners were diverted to hear him explain, in answer to a question about his personal life, that his pastimes included "middle-aged antics", and they must have wondered what innocent japes – or perhaps amorous frolics – the old boy got up to, until they worked out that *middle-aged* was his very reasonable attempt at translating *du moyen age* (medieval), and that *antics* was his Gallic stress pattern for 'antiques'.

That French speakers of English may present special difficulties is a fact unacknowledged in parts of the media. When, in July 1987, Britain's (independent) Channel 4 Television screened part of a world-wide documentary series on mountain-climbing in Patagonia, the producers chose to use a French commentator who was almost a caricature of the incomprehensible Frenchman.

The inability of most British people to utter more than a few words of mispronounced French – or indeed any foreign language – is part of international folklore based on observable fact. But the French are hardly better. I write as a speaker of French, I love the French people, and greatly admire French culture. But I have to admit that most French people, if they speak English at all, speak it atrociously, and often seem to take a chauvinistic delight in doing so. The British fail to learn other people's languages partly because they are insular, and partly because their motivation to do so is reduced by the ability – indeed the eagerness – of most other nations in the world to learn English. (When it comes to selling goods to those nations, the British lack of linguistic versatility becomes a serious handicap.) Most British schoolchildren learn a bit of French, typically for about two or three years, with depressing results. More than 80 per cent of French schoolchildren in state schools, and over 90 per cent in private schools, choose English as their first foreign language, and learn it for considerably longer than their British counterparts learn French, though at the hands of teachers the most prestigious of whom tend to be qualified in English literary criticism rather than in English language, and least of all perhaps in *spoken* English. In contrast to the situation in England, the efforts of teachers in France are given strong support outside the classroom by their pupils' access to media material in English, especially the language of popular music. The whole effort of learning English in France is, however, compromised by a long-drawn-out nostalgia for the days when French was still *the* international language, and by frenzied attempts to protect French from inevitable contamination by English. Italians and Spaniards, whose own languages impose obstacles similar to French in the matter of pronouncing English, have comparable problems of intelligibility, but we simply do not meet such speakers in any number unless we go abroad, whereas the French and their fractured English accents have been our close neighbours for many hundreds of years.

The ways in which different home-grown accents, as opposed to those of foreign speakers of English, are used on radio and television both reflect and reinforce similar reactions involving intelligibility, distraction, and prejudice. Of the great volume of letters received by the BBC, a substantial proportion every week offer observations, and more generally criticisms, of speakers' accents – letters of the "I've had it up to here with the Welsh and the Irish" kind, and protests like that concerning the former choice of Michael Parkinson, who has a slight Yorkshire accent, as the presenter of Radio 4's popular and long-running series *Desert Island Discs*, on the scarcely credible grounds that the listener couldn't understand what he was saying. As Professor Peter Trudgill, now of Essex University, a leading expert on language variety, always insists, the claim of unintelligibility is often a cover for mere accent prejudice, because "it is no longer socially acceptable to criticize somebody because of their accent". Yet both intelligibility and distraction may be very real problems with accents spoken with any degree of *breadth* on the media.

When Susan Rae left Radio Scotland in the early 1980s to become an announcer on BBC Radio's main national programme broadcast from London, she was surprised at the reaction her accent provoked. "For the first time I was made to feel very Scottish, not having been terribly aware of it before. Listeners seem to have flocked to their telephones and typewriters as soon as I hit the airwaves. They either loved or loathed me . . . Some of them were very depressing, in fact, and the kind of thing was, 'Many of the sounds uttered by Miss Rae are incomprehensible' – and that's typical of a lot of the more negative ones." Nor has the 'hate mail' stopped coming. "People write to me to say, 'Please don't take this personally . . .': they then proceed to say how much they hate me, how much they hate my accent, and then tell me to get back to the hills and the heather."

Susan Rae ascribes this sort of attitude to a mixture of xenophobia, snobbishness, and English insularity – "I don't think I'm all that hard to understand" – but this shows a lack of awareness of some real problems which the accents of Scots can produce. In many varieties of Scottish English it is impossible to distinguish, as other English accents can, between the sounds of *dose* and *doze, baize* and *base, pulling* and *pooling*. Susan Rae's accent has some of these features: it also merges *collar* and *caller*, and in an item on prize dogs at Crufts in 1986 her apparent reference to the dogs' *honours* cloaked, for non-Scottish ears, an intended reference to the dogs' *owners*. On another occasion her announcement of the forthcoming *Foot Programme* dealt neither with chiropody nor the shoe trade: the subject was food, which has a shorter vowel in Scottish English. To do her justice, her accent does show some signs of modification – whether conscious or unconscious – in the direction of RP (even the longer RP *a* in *forecast*), but Scotticisms such as *genu-wine* (for genuine) seem to be asserting the opposite tendency.

One of the indices of real breadth in a Scots accent, and of predictable comprehension difficulties for non-Scottish listeners, is the Scottish *r*. Words like *world* and *cart* are a test of this. If the Scottish speaker makes such words sound like two syllables (which may make *cart* difficult to distinguish from *carrot*) he or she can expect incomprehension, or at the least distraction, to result. BBC radio's newsreader James Alexander Gordon, disc jockey Ken Bruce, and BBC's television presenter Magnus Magnusson, all pass this test with flying colours, while retaining an obvious Scottish identity. Indeed, in Scotland itself most BBC newsreaders use an RP accent or something close to it, so that it is not surprising that a pupil in a Scottish school should identify the accent known as the 'Queen's English' as, "It's how the guy on the BBC will talk." Lady (Isobel) Barnett, a famous television personality of the 1960s, grew up with a noticeable version of the educated Glasgow accent. When she appeared on BBC television nationally she had adapted to a paralect of RP, in keeping with the image she wanted to project and the wider audience she wanted to address.

When broad Scottish accents are heard on national radio and TV programmes in Britain, for example in interviews with sportsmen or disaster witnesses, there are formidable comprehension problems. Footballer Kenny Dalgleish, interviewed on television after Liverpool's victory in the Cup Final in May 1986, should have been provided with an interpreter, or the interview furnished with subtitles. A miner's union leader at Kinneil colliery, interviewed on BBC Radio's *Today* programme in 1982; a Scottish van driver interviewed for an item on hypermarkets for the BBC's *Money Programme* in 1985; a Scottish holidaymaker interviewed for BBC's television news during the killer heatwave in Athens in July 1987 – these are all examples of the same incomprehensibility. After the Glaswegian Teddy Taylor migrated from a Glasgow constituency to represent one in the South of England, his fellow-conservative MP Julian Critchley described him in the *Observer* as delivering his robust views "in an incomprehensible accent". Critchley was obviously teasing, for Taylor's moderate Scottish accent features pose no problems of intelligibility, though they probably have power to distract. But in the immediate aftermath of the Zeebrugge ferry disaster in March 1987, when radio and television reports tried to give the public some idea of what it was like to be on board when the vessel keeled over, the greater part of a description by a soldier who survived, delivered on BBC radio, was rendered unintelligible to millions by a broad Scottish accent. Jimmy

Knapp, who comes from Kilmarnock and is General Secretary of the National Union of Railwaymen, has the same kind of difficulty when he is interviewed about rail strikes, etc. on TV and radio news bulletins.

The fact that nearly half a million people living in England were born in Scotland ought to accustom the English to Scottish accents, but the number of complaints voiced about "the amount of Scottishness heard on BBC Radio 4" suggest that this is a slow process. Furthermore, the Scottish accent is remarkably resilient. All over England there are pockets of Scottishness, in places like Corby (Northants) and Coalville (Leicestershire), where a close-knit community of immigrants maintain this badge of their ethnic identity. In 1986 I was introduced to a young man of eighteen from Derby in the north Midlands who spoke with a Scottish accent. He explained that his large family had moved down from a town near Glasgow when he was only seven, and the speech of his many elder brothers and sisters had helped sustain his Scottish accent despite attendance at local Derbyshire schools. Moreover, he emphasized, he was determined to retain this Scottish accent even though, as he claimed, he frequently had to repeat what he said *ten times* before he was understood.

Ireland – both Northern and Southern – furnishes the media with many accents, though it is doubtful whether the majority of listeners can distinguish between those two main varieties. The English spoken in the Republic of Ireland has various degrees of overlay of the native Gaelic language which is being kept alive at enormous cost. The Northern Ireland accent shows the influences of Gaelic and, even more, of Scottish English. Listeners in the rest of the United Kingdom probably perceive the Ulster accent as represented by three kinds of voice, for which we may take as examples the Revd Dr Ian Paisley, MP; the long-serving BBC political correspondent John Cole; and the interviewer and presenter of a light-music programme, Gloria Hunniford. Such perceptions are not a serious misrepresentation of the broad system of Northern Ireland accents. Dr Paisley's accent is close to the urban vernacular of Belfast, and at the far extreme from the most educated Ulster speaker whose model is not RP but the educated local standard in some ways comparable with the educated standard in Scotland. This fact, his lack of conventional educational qualifications (despite the 'Dr'), and the inability to modulate his public-speaking voice, combine with the content of his political and religious utterances to sustain a stereotype of what his critics have variously described as a "hate-filled rabble-rouser", a "music-hall joke", and a "man with all the spirituality of a rhinoceros, and none of the mystery". His accent is regularly made the subject of ridicule by the satirical magazine *Private Eye* ("anti-Chraste", "thorty paces of sulver", etc.).

There are varieties of urban Ulster accent much more densely incomprehensible than Dr Paisley's, however. When they are heard on the mainland by listeners to documentaries on aspects of the sectarian conflict in Northern Ireland – as in the voice of a repentant ex-gunman on a religious programme, or a witness to some new terrorist outrage on a news programme – the resultant bafflement "adds to the sinister air"; as one radio critic put it, "It is unsettling not to understand half of what one of your compatriots is saying." Young men are particularly assertive in maintaining this urban vernacular; as elsewhere, it is women who aspire to the standard accent, and, for all Northern Irelanders who want to move towards RP there are elocution and drama classes where such tuition is available. The power of the stereotype of the broad Belfast accent is evident in the report of a *Sunday Times* investigation in 1983 into a stolen-car racket in Ulster involving a Mr Platt. The newspaper used its Northern Ireland correspondent, Chris Ryder, who was able on the phone to turn on an accent appropriate to the Belfast dealer who he was pretending to be. "His heavy Irish accent seemed to convince Platt of his bona fides as a corrupt punter", and by this deception the racket was exposed.

The accent in which the BBC's John Cole delivers his commentaries on political events represents an intermediate Ulster variety compatible with educatedness but still very markedly Ulster. To my particular set of prejudices it is completely acceptable, and with greater familiarity I no longer find it distracting, but others are not willing to allow it the same indulgence. Throughout the 1980s *Private Eye* has carried a regular spoof item ridiculing his accent, in a series interrupted only briefly when John Cole was seriously ill. It usually contains a phrase like "hondootedly Mossis Thotcher" (undoubtedly Mrs Thatcher . . .). One would have thought that by now any traces of humour in this exercise would have evaporated, but some readers presumably find it funny. I was surprised recently while watching a BBC news bulletin in the company of a group of young people who had evinced no strong prejudices on accents and who were not readers of *Private Eye*, to find that they too reacted spontaneously against Mr Cole's accent. On the other hand, journalist and politician Woodrow Wyatt recently wrote in a review that Cole "is blessed with an attractive Northern Ireland accent which, together with his questing face, makes him a friendly, doggy figure." Many professional men and women on the British mainland have this kind of educated but still strong Ulster accent, and it in no way prejudices their professional acceptability as would, for example, a broad Cockney or a broad Glasgow vernacular accent. Dr John Bodkin Adams, sensationally acquitted in 1957 of hastening the deaths of his rich, elderly Eastbourne patients, had such an accent. According to an obituarist, "His practice thrived in a town of quiet gentility where a number of wealthy elderly women relied on the soft burr of the sympathetic bachelor doctor to ease the discomforts of their old age."

Our third exemplar, Gloria Hunniford, represents a variety of Northern Ireland accent whose Ulster features make it broader than an RP paralect although it is still close to RP. It is the variety most acceptable on the British mainland, and in Ms Hunniford's case is an important ingredient of her charm as a broadcaster. It conjures up an image of Ulster, yet not of the harsh Ulster of sectarian bigotry and violence, but rather of a basically gentle, tolerant, and compassionate people. It helps us forget the cruel divisions of a province where Catholics and Protestants can often identify each other by their speech forms: by the distinctive use of idiom, by accent traces, and most specifically by the pronunciation of the letter *h* in the alphabet, which in Catholic schools is traditionally taught as *haitch* and in Protestant schools as *aitch*, though the typical Ulster vowel in both words is slightly different from RP (and closer to the e in *egg*).

Southern Irish accents represent a broader spectrum, though this breadth is not reflected in the voices heard on the British media. Irish 'character' parts may tend to use an accent feature which is common to all social classes, even the more educated, within the Republic: the distinctive Irish *th*, which is often pronounced as *t*, giving *thanks* the same sound as *tanks*; or pronounced as a sound very close to *t*, in words like *with*. But this and other very distinctive Southern Irish features are barely hinted at in the speech of those whose 'Irish brogues' – consisting often of the merest traces of Irishness – are well represented on British radio and television, and when they appear in the speech of (say) surgeons, academics, or novelists in England, are usually regarded as an ingredient of the speaker's charm. The number of British media personalities whose career success may be connected with this accent is large – the comedian Dave Allen, Frank Delaney, Val Doonican, the late Eamonn Andrews, Henry Kelly and – king of them all – Terry Wogan. Wogan's success may relate to the closeness of his Irish accent to RP: sometimes it is barely perceptible, at other times he will pronounce 'ducks' as 'docks' and thus remind us of his Irishness. Henry Kelly has retained, as did also Eamonn Andrews, a much more obvious Irish accent. The possible reasons for the acceptability of this accent on the British media will be discussed later in the chapter.

Pattie Caldwell speaks with a variety of Lancashire accent,

which did not prevent her achieving prominence as the presenter of a BBC Radio 4 programme of interviews on current issues called *You and Yours*, though according to some listeners it should have done. Her early appearances on BBC radio were greeted by a torrent of complaints and some really nasty abuse, though when she mentioned this on the air there were also many people who wrote in to assure her that they were quite happy with her accent.

Lancashire accents are generally around the middle of the hierarchy of accent acceptability in England. But what happens to media figures who speak with accents from the bottom of the pecking order, like broad Cockney? To start with, not many such speakers find their way into regular broadcasting positions. Lorraine Chase was used to do part of the radio commentary on the wedding of the Prince of Wales and Lady Diana Spencer in 1981. According to one critic, she "sounded like someone playing a demented stage Cockney – shrieking about 'geezers in red' " (the second division of the Sovereign's escort). But perhaps she spoke for many more listeners than her critics allowed when she commented, "I was just a bit upset 'e didn't give 'er a smacker in the church" – *just*, *bit*, and *upset* all subject to the London glottalling treatment of *t*.

For "statuesque Cockney starlet Janet Street-Porter" (the description is *Private Eye*'s) her accent has been a mixed blessing. As a television presenter and media personality it has been her most obvious trade mark. But, she complains, "The British are so obsessed with labelling people. I mean, they think I must be working class, they think I must be *thick*." Unintelligent she certainly is not, and her academic qualifications in structural mechanics entitle her to resent the labels so unthinkingly fastened on her. Whether she is entitled to real surprise when, as she claims, in the Members' Enclosure at Goodwood racecourse she was jeered by a group of 'Sloane Rangers' for her accent, is another matter, since she must be aware of the social conventions which operate in that kind of place more than anywhere else.

A selection of the prejudices of *Private Eye* has already been noted, so it was predictable that a journal founded, and run in its early years, by old boys of one particular public school (Shrewsbury) – Richard Ingrams, Christopher Booker, and Paul Foot – should have given a nickname such as "Sid Yobbo" to the 'professional Cockney', Derek Jameson, who in 1986 took over a prime weekday-morning slot on BBC's Radio 2 which had earlier been the medium by which Terry Wogan had achieved fame. Introducing records, keeping up a stream of patter, conducting short interviews, and reading out pieces from newspapers – some of the more 'popular' of which he once edited – are the stuff of Jameson's performance: what a *Guardian* writer called "tabloid journalism on the air". "Of course it isn't a real Cockney accent – I can turn it on, being from Hackney," he explained to the *Sunday Telegraph*. To a *Sunday Times* columnist it is "that extraordinary voice". The initial public reaction came in the form of 1,971 letters and phone calls, "most of them uncomplimentary", but he also had a substantial number of supporters, like the one who commented on his "warm, friendly voice". He himself is said to see "his Cockney street-trader voice" as "a breakthrough for democracy".

Initial audience reaction to Derek Jameson's assumption of office was an increase of half a million listeners to his programme. Critics would claim that this kind of audience appeal is comparable to the vulgarization by which the *Sun* and more recently the *Star* – and perhaps even the *News of the World* under Jameson's own editorship – increased their circulation figures. Certainly Jameson's style seems to confirm a great number of prejudices about this kind of 'popular' London accent. Clarity is at a discount. "We'll arst her," he will say: then stumbling over his announcement of a song with the words Hickory Hollers in the title, "I can't say all those *h*s." His *-ing* suffixes are uncertain, so *singing* may come out as *singin'* and as *singing* in the same sentence, and why not? As he admits, it isn't a *real* Cockney accent. What he calls *craw* and *jaws* turn out to mean 'cruel' and 'jewels'. He has a struggle with the pronunciation of long words like 'tumultuous': he "stresses syllables that no voice has stressed before"; and some literate idiomatic expressions emerge in garbled form. Referring to some of the duties the royal family have been called upon to perform at various times, he adds, "and no more so during the war years", leaving his listeners to work out the intended meaning as, "and *never* more so *than* during the war years".

"I was born ignorant," declared Jameson on a television programme in 1987. Another interviewer says that he is "haunted by his background", and that his accent is a "grim, dreadful reminder" of the poverty, illegitimacy, and experience of reform school which scarred his early life.

Britain is full of people who have triumphed over humble beginnings and made successes in various ways of their lives. The apparent radio popularity of Derek Jameson is depressing to those who care about language because it confirms the associations between a widely spoken variety of London accent and a self-proclaimed ignorance, anti-educatedness, and an inability to handle accurately the more literate forms of the spoken word. Though the use of the Cockney character actor Arthur Mullard as an occasional chairman of a serious radio discussion programme *Midweek* produced a flood of hostile comment from listeners, it is refreshing that there should be a change from what one listener called "pretentious waffle from middle-class voices". But the media will only do justice to the dignity of the most disfavoured non-standard accents when they use speakers of these varieties who are also able to articulate clearly and to handle the grammar, idiom, and intonation of literate speech adequately. Otherwise all the factors of unintelligibility, distraction and, above all, prejudice are likely to come into play simultaneously.

Much of the characterization of the fictional content of radio and television serves further to confirm the stereotyping of accents. The most famous of all British soap operas to date, Granada's *Coronation Street*, has been running since 1960 with a following that made its fictional characters national figures in Britain, and has mediated a view of British northern working-class life and values to many people across the world. Though all of its regular characters reflect the accent (and some of the dialect) of urban Lancashire, there is no evidence that this accent or dialect has influenced the rest of the nation. As Robert McCrum has put it, we've been watching *Coronation Street* for a generation, but we don't all say "Tarrah". In fact, though, there is not a great deal that is distinctive about the vocabulary, grammar, or idiom of *Coronation Street*, as Jeffrey Miller's guide to "Street Talk" (1986) shows. "Mushy peas for tea and nowt for afters", only has one word (nowt) which is not common to most British vernaculars, and 90 per cent of the words or phrases listed in that book are familiar to all speakers of colloquial English. Though millions of us now know, as a result of this series, that *any road* is a northern variant of *anyway*, standard English and the RP accent exert greater influence on the residents of Coronation Streets all over the North than does their dialect or accent on us.

The characterization of *Coronation Street* is interesting. For most of the series's life, the broadest local accents have been allocated to characters like Stan and Hilda Ogden, she a naive but nosey-parker charwoman with her hair in curlers all day long, he a manual worker of exceptional slow-wittedness. Accents closest to RP have been represented by Ken Barlow, who is portrayed as having trained as a teacher and who has often been called upon to exercise some kind of leadership role in the local community, and by the former landlady of the Rover's Return, Annie Walker, a brilliantly observed character in whom well-spokenness was allied to a yearning for respectability that was not without traces of snobbery.

Brookside, a TV soap opera which plays to a much smaller audience on the minority commercial Channel 4, is set in a private housing estate in the Liverpool area, and though its characters tend to follow the stereotype of the more educated professionals speaking in varying degrees of approximation to RP, the series is unusual in that some of its other characters offer one of the few regular opportunities on the national media to hear Scouse in any degree of breadth.

EastEnders, the success story of the 1980s, is the BBC's recent answer to *Coronation Street* in the battle of the 'soaps'. It was launched in 1985, and at times has achieved audiences of 27 million viewers; more commonly an episode will be seen by around 17 million. As its title suggests, its location is in the East End of London, among lower-class people, some with strong local roots, others more recent immigrants. The predominant flavour of the dialogue is 'popular' London speech, though there are few signs of full-blown Cockney, whose special vocabulary (including extensive rhyming slang) and very distinctive vowel and consonant changes would make the series incomprehensible outside a narrow radius of London. The purest RP speakers are Asians (including an Asian doctor) and the area manager of a chain of breweries, who for good measure is given a double-barrelled name.

There is nothing in these soap operas which does anything to challenge – indeed anything other than confirm – the stereotype which associates certain accents with educatedness and career opportunity, and others with the lack of these. In *Brookside* in 1984 a mother was represented as recoiling from the reported indiscipline of the local comprehensive school and in consequence seeking admission for her sons at a private school, where they at first fail the entrance exam because, she claims, they do not speak with the right accents. After confronting the headmaster, she obtains their admission as weekly boarders: boarding schools, as we know, have greater power to change accents than day schools. And from an episode of *EastEnders* in April 1985 the lesson was conveyed that a posh accent serves to secure its owner prompter attention from Social Security officials.

Some interesting messages about accents and schooling are conveyed by *Grange Hill*, a well-established and long-running television series set in a comprehensive school, with credible characters, a good story-line, and generally excellent acting by the children concerned. Some of the episodes are of outstanding quality. The realism with which the series handles problems such as truancy, indiscipline, bullying, protection rackets among pupils, and drugs, makes it a taboo programme in some homes, and a *bête noire* among some parents, though such hostility simply makes it all the more enjoyable to the huge number of children who do manage to watch it. It is noticeable that in some episodes teachers are openly mocked by pupils for having RP accents, and the son of an RP-speaking solicitor is represented as having acquired a vernacular accent through attendance at this comprehensive school.

The media treatment of accent variation is further displayed in the particular functions it allocates to the speakers of different accents in its news and information programmes. National radio news bulletins are conventionally read by RP speakers, confirming the widely accepted assumption that the authority of a message is enhanced by its being spoken in RP. The traces of marked RP which were common among BBC newsreaders until the 1950s are now rare, though Independent Television News has one newscaster with a hyperlectal *o*. Alistair Stewart often says *say-viet* (Soviet), *frazen* (frozen), *pray-test* (protest), and *explaysion* (explosion). Two BBC newsreaders of recent years, Angela Rippon and Jan Leeming, shared an idiosyncrasy which caused distraction and a certain amount of ridicule, in their over-exact pronunciation of foreign names of persons and places. In modern British English, the rule for the pronunciation of a foreign name is that if a version of the name entered the language some hundreds of years ago, it is pronounced as an English word: Paris, Geneva, Florence, Munich, Lisbon, and so on. Otherwise, names are given an *Anglicized* approximation to the foreign pronunciation. Rather strained attempts at 'authentic' versions of names like Mugabe and Nkomo excited much satirical comment.

Minor idiosyncrasies do not necessarily reduce the effectiveness of a newscaster, for research in the USA has shown that the more memorable the news presenter, the better the viewer retains what he or she is saying. But authority and credibility seem to demand that the memorability factor should not extend beyond the frontiers of a standard accent. Once established, such an aura of authority has huge commercial potential; it is reported that the BBC's Frank Bough (of the Breakfast television programme), John Humphreys (a TV newsreader and later a presenter on the daily current affairs radio programme *Today*), and Nick Ross of the crime-busting *Crimewatch*, can supplement their regular salaries by earning up to £2,000 a day doing promotional and training videos for big companies.

Certain voices and accents have the power to offer comfort and reassurance, and establish trust. In 1983 it was written of Patricia Hughes, an announcer on the BBC's 'serious' music programme Radio 3, that, "When she presents a concert, baffling names and obscure music suddenly become manageable, almost promising. When she reads the news, horrible events appear somehow less ugly." Her voice and diction were described as traditional: "English well spoken is beautiful," she herself said firmly. "I do mind about it very much. A slightly 'off' sound – a sloppy voice – is ugly and I don't like it . . . ; an overdone upper-class voice is quite awful too." An elderly lady who died in 1985 left a small sum in her will to two BBC television newsreaders "as a small token of my appreciation of the way the news is read". The BBC World Service has a special reputation for the careful choice of accents in which its news bulletins and other informational programmes are read. When a British journalist was recently allowed, exceptionally, to pay a visit to long-isolated Albania, and actually given a chance to meet a few Albanians, he found himself talking to one whose English accent had been acquired during hours of listening to the BBC's World

Service. Millions of people across the world show evidence in their spoken English of the same influence.

On other radio programmes, however, RP and the educated standard accents of Scotland, Wales, and Ireland can claim no monopoly of authority or eloquence. John Arlott, broadcaster and journalist, joined the BBC as a producer of poetry programmes in 1945; then, the following year, by a happy accident he began the cricket commentaries which were to make his voice one of the best-known in the world of sport for a quarter of a century. Yet the rich Hampshire accent was nearly lost to the nation in 1948, when the head of Outside Broadcasting told him, "You have an interesting mind, but a vulgar voice." He had just begun the process of trying to adjust his accent when the well-known BBC actor Valentine Dyall dissuaded him with the threat to "cut his tongue out" if he persisted. He later claimed that his accent had "reduced a little" because he no longer lived in the Basingstoke of his boyhood, but some people would say the opposite – that he made the most of every nuance of an accent so expressive of the English countryside, the village green in summer, and the drowsy murmur of spectators' conversation. But, in general, the accents used in broadcast sports commentaries reflect the social class image of the sport concerned, with tennis and show-jumping often using commentators with marked-RP accents, and soccer a variety of standard and non-standard accents. Cricket, with its tradition of 'gentlemen' and 'players', is served by a mix of hyperlectal and plebeian accents.

I am one of those people who, while loving parks and flowers, loathe everything else to do with gardening. Yet for many years I listened whenever I could to the BBC radio programme *Gardeners' Question Time*. Its fascination lay in two factors: the accents of the three original panellists (two Northcountrymen, Fred Loads and Bill Sowerbutts, and a Scot, Professor Alan Gemmell) and the opportunity to hear experts with a great amount of scientific knowledge and practical experience, as well as a lot of earthy wisdom, arguing about their expertise. Here were the accents of a real kind of authority founded upon personal competence.

But the Lancashire accent – and the wisdom – of Fred Loads and his like have been restricted to a narrow range of functions on national radio and television programmes. Scottish, Northern Ireland, North and West Country accents are tolerable in gardening programmes and common among weather-forecasters, but it is noticeable that this tolerance does not extend to the most disfavoured urban accents associated with London, Birmingham, Glasgow, Liverpool, and Belfast. Comedians are among the few who are allowed to use the whole range of accents including – indeed especially – the disfavoured ones. This applies both to stand-up comics and to characters in situation comedies: a non-standard accent, or, better still, the ability to handle a number of such accents, is an important part of the comedian's stock-in-trade. Most of the humour, and the credibility, of television series like *Only Fools and Horses, Auf Wiedersehen Pet*, and *Bread*, would be lost without the strong flavour of Cockney, Geordie, or Scouse in the voices of the main characters. It is not as great a surprise to us as it appears to be to Janet Street-Porter that people should assume that her Cockney accent must indicate that she is what she calls "a cheery kinda person". "Lots of people expect me to instantly tell them a joke just because I've got this kinda accent, and they're dead disappointed when I can't."

The casting of characters in plays and films on radio and television reflects the same stereotypical assumptions. As a lady from Bournville complained in a letter to the *Observer* in 1981, Birmingham accents are invariably used for the villains – the 'baddies'. If a non-standard accent is ever used for a kindly, lovable person, a 'goodie', it will often be a soft Irish or Welsh one.

Advertising on television carries these assumptions even further. There is extraordinarily little use of non-standard accents in TV commercials, which is all the more remarkable in that independent television, which is funded by advertising, operates on a regional basis. Scottish television and commercial radio stations put out most of their commercials in RP, the most obvious exception being advertisements for certain brands of beer, for which the essential 'macho' image dictates a heavy non-standard accent. Commercial television and radio on Merseyside use Scouse accents for very few products. When non-standard accents are indeed used on nationwide commercials, it is often in the humorous context which advertising agencies advise is one of the best ways to gain viewers' attention and to mitigate the boredom of frequently repeated advertisements. After the Japanese car firm Nissan had established a new factory in Sunderland near Tyneside, it spent £3 million on a national television advertising campaign in 1987 using a commercial "intended to be amusing and to grab the attention". It showed a Geordie car worker travelling to and from Japan extolling Nissan's virtues in such a broad local accent that it required an interpretation in English by a Japanese. The local engineering union passed a formal resolution condemning the commercial, which workers felt ridiculed the people of Sunderland and was harmful to the image of the North-East.

Comic, yokel, villain: these are the most powerful images of non-standard accent speakers promoted by the media. Labour MP and former academic Austin Mitchell has summarized some of the ways in which non-standard accents are perceived by the rest of the nation:

> The Liverpool accent became the symbol of the new brutalism. The Cockney accent bespoke the shrewd operator, Yorkshire blunt talking was the tongue of the new men of power trying to conceal their duplicity behind bluff, honest exteriors. Yet the Geordie's dulcet tones remain comic, quaintly symbolic of an old backwardness.

Liverpool Scouse's ability to "symbolize the new brutalism" was enhanced by a television commercial transmitted nationally in

September 1987, one of the new breed using the realism of 'shock-horror' methods to warn against the dangers of Aids. In it, junkies injecting themselves with drugs had Scouse accents.

But Dr Mitchell does not deny that the image may reflect a depressing reality, that the Geordie accent and dialect may represent "the verbal side of dominant working-class culture" in the North-East which is "insulated, isolated, rough and tough". For this is, he says, "the most drunken, most violent part of the nation: Geordie crime, violence, delinquency and wife-beating are high", and, as the writer John Ardagh has observed, Geordies treat their women in an almost Muslim manner.* Nor can it be denied that reactions to the broadest Glasgow accents may be a realistic appraisal of the culture of a city where, according to another writer in the *Sunday Times*, "deprivation, despair, casual violence and religious bigotry go hand in hand with pride, warmth, humour and deep humanity."

Outsiders' evaluations, fair or unfair, do not prevent local pride. 'I belong to Glasgae' is sung with passionate loyalty, and in similar ways Cockneys and Liverpudlians proudly proclaim their identity. But *nobody celebrates the Birmingham accent*. Neither regional BBC nor independent television based on Birmingham, nor local radio stations, employ speakers with authentic full-blown Birmingham accents as newsreaders, programme presenters, or even weather-forecasters. This accent, with its often nasalized mix of Cockney and 'northern' vowels, is not used for commercials on radio or TV. In May 1986 Central ITV, sited in Birmingham, carried a British Rail commercial advertising cheap inter-city day trips from Birmingham: the accent used in the commercial was Liverpool! The radio critic of a national Sunday newspaper reported in 1981 on a BBC programme about the shooting of a pregnant girl: "It happened

* These characterizations of the Geordie image must be set against the fact that some of the evaluation experiments reported have tended to put the Geordie *accent* in a much more favourable category than Scouse, Cockney, Birmingham and Glaswegian.

in Birmingham ... Almost everyone spoke in flat, nasal, Midlands English, *the most depressing accent in the kingdom.*"

Yet the efforts of local radio and television organizers to diversify the accents used by their newsreaders and presenters – and thus possibly to modify these stereotypes – are compromised by a major difficulty. Within the past two decades Britain has become covered by networks not only of regional commercial TV channels (and by stations offering regional programmes for the BBC) but also of BBC and commercial radio stations, so that most large towns are within reach of a local radio service (and perhaps two) as well as two television channels which offer regional material. A local radio or television station has no difficulty in recruiting staff with the accent of that locality who can conduct interviews and keep up bright and breezy patter while introducing pop records. The problem comes when such speakers are called upon, as they have to be, to read news bulletins, press reviews, and other information-content items, written in standard English.

Finding speakers with local accents rather than RP often means that such announcers are of limited levels of formal education and are unfamiliar with the characteristic intonation and phrasing patterns of reading aloud in standard English, with its different idioms, vocabulary, verb and preposition systems, and its differential uses of adverbs and adjectives. It cannot be their fault if their diction is poor, since no one offers training in the diction of the Birmingham accent, and even fewer experts offer elocution lessons in the 'popular' London accent than the small number who can teach 'stage Cockney'.

Travelling round the country tuned in on the car radio, I have come to regard as commonplace on local radio pronunciations such as *hair* for *heir* in a news item; *grievous* made to rhyme with *devious*; '*catrastophic*' for catastrophic and 'conno-sewer' for connoisseur. General knowledge of place names and proper names is limited, so we get 'Ile' in Isleworth, and Schofield becomes 'Showfield'. "We'll have *more fuller* updates after the

9 a.m. news", was a promise of further travel information during severe winter weather by a local radio announcer in January 1987. It was a Midlands television presenter who introduced a programme about a museum of household implements with the comment that "Modern-day kitchen utensils tend to be *somewhat rather* bland." "Tracey has wrote to me", was the way a BBC local radio announcer introduced a record request; on another occasion he made such a muddle of a common idiomatic expression in standard English while reading a review of the national press that he broke off with "or something like that anyway".

Similar mishandling of standard pronunciations or grammatical usage can sometimes be heard from RP speakers on national radio and television programmes, but on these local programmes they are a daily, sometimes hourly, occurrence, predictable because of the unfamiliar cadences of the standard English they are called upon to read out, and their own limited experience of education. The overall effect is to emphasize the dissociation between educatedness and the possession of one of the non-standard (especially urban) accents of *England*. (Scotland, Ireland, and to a limited extent Wales are, as we saw in Chapter Five, a different case in having an educated variety of regional accent.)

"Accents that don't hit the right note can screech over the air like razor blades on glass," wrote a newspaper's radio critic in 1986. There are limits, as we have seen, to the radio and television authorities' scope for using non-standard accents, and to the functions for which they can be used. The uneven pattern of exposure which results has caused the journalist Miles Kington to ask, "Did you realize that you find it easier to understand your American cousins than your cousins in Newcastle, Belfast, or Glasgow?" According to *The Times* diary column in 1986, BBC Radio 4's presentation editor, himself a Liverpudlian, decided, after experimenting with the use of regional accents, that Scouse and Geordie are still not acceptable for national radio. But in general we should welcome the wider range of accents heard in recent years, especially when it challenges the stereotypes associated with specific non-standard accents rather than confirms them, as it does in the case of Derek Jameson on BBC Radio 2 and a number of speakers used on local radio and television.

Meanwhile there is an interesting pointer in the current popularity, noticed earlier in this chapter, of certain soft Southern Irish accents heard on chat shows and in interviews of an intellectually not very exacting nature. The 'ethnic' identity they reveal is gentle and unassertive, rather than strident (as certain Scottish accents on radio are felt to be). Standing outside the British social system, they are relatively classless. They are, in fact, a perfect vehicle for an interminable stream of effortless but innocuous drivel, which is what viewers seem to want from such chat shows, and listeners expect from presenters of pop music programmes. Since I see no potential rivals in sight from among other accents of the British Isles, I predict that the popularity of such speakers will continue, and that intending applicants waiting to cross the Irish Sea can expect a promising future.

SEVEN

The accents of politics

In Canada, the Progressive Conservative party, one of the two dominant political parties in national politics, acquired a new leader in 1983. He was completely unknown outside Canada, he had limited political experience, he had never held office as a government minister nor even sat as an MP. What was decisive in carrying Brian Mulroney, a lawyer and business executive, to the leadership of his party and thus to the position of Prime Minister of Canada – to which he was swept in 1984 by the largest parliamentary majority in Canadian history – was the set of qualities he had shown as a performer on the mass media, especially television. Among such performances were his much-publicized role as a lawyer in a quasi-prosecuting role in a famous commission inquiring into labour union corruption, and his previous bid for political leadership which had focused national attention on his good looks, his mellifluous voice and – as with J. F. Kennedy and Neil Kinnock – his very attractive wife.

The ability of television to make and break politicians has been one of the critical developments in the political history of the free world in the past few decades. It is not without significance that the man elected President of the United States in 1980 and 1984 was a former film actor, though he was, of course, much more than that. But Ronald Reagan's gifts as a communicator, and specifically the use he made, as president, of television as a means of addressing the nation, were accounted one of the great strengths which helped him maintain his popularity despite several major political reverses. By contrast, his Democratic opponent in the 1984 presidential election, Walter Mondale, accounted for his failure as follows: "Politics today requires a mastery of television. I never really warmed to it and it never really warmed to me."

The ability to exploit the mass media of the spoken word was recognized early by F. D. Roosevelt who pioneered in the 1930s a controversial style in addressing the US nation, and by Winston Churchill whose radio speeches to Britain and the world now have their place in history. Television and technical advances have together brought the new factors of immediacy, visibility, spontaneity, informality, and saturation coverage. Winston Churchill's oratorical dominance of the House of Commons was based upon meticulously prepared speeches in which even the apparent hesitations and spontaneous asides were elaborately rehearsed. It is doubtful whether he would have had anything like the same success in the cut and thrust of searching television interviews and studio mini-debates with opposing political leaders. He also had a minor speech peculiarity – some of his *s*'s came out as *sh* – whose constant exposure might have made him vulnerable to satirists: one can visualize a weekly mocking paragraph in *Private Eye*.

Clement Attlee, leader of the great reforming Labour government of 1945–50, would, in an age of television politics, have been a non-starter. He could be devastatingly effective as chairman of his Cabinet and he had many strong qualifications to lead his party and government, but he had a thin, unimpressive speaking voice and often sounded ineffective in public. At Cambridge University in the 1950s, I was present at an epic confrontation in the student debating society, the Cambridge Union, when Attlee debated with the Liberal peer Lord Beveridge (whose famous Report provided the blueprint for the Welfare State), on the issues of liberalism versus socialism. Though Attlee was adequate in formal debate, in the Union's committee room afterwards when the animated discussion continued in a small group, I stood and marvelled at the ex-Prime Minister's inability to secure attention for what he was trying to say.

Harold Macmillan, who became Prime Minister in 1957, was perhaps the first British political leader to perceive the opportunities of television, which at that date had only recently achieved a mass audience in Britain. Though, as we have seen in Chapter Three, Macmillan's accent had hyperlectal features to which the mass of the British public have become increasingly unsympathetic, some of his television appearances were regarded as very successful, even if some viewers might have been put off by the whiff of old-world Tory privilege which his voice and manner conveyed.

When Sir Keith Joseph stood down as Secretary of State for Education and Science towards the end of Mrs Thatcher's second government in 1986, there was prolonged speculation about who would succeed him. A BBC political correspondent reported on Radio 4 that Kenneth Baker was regarded by Conservative MPs as the likeliest choice "because he is seen as the best communicator", and he was subsequently appointed to an office which put a high premium on his communicative talents. But if television shows some politicians off to good effect, it is unkind to others. The *Observer*'s Alan Watkins, doyen of British political commentators, said on BBC Radio 4 that both Sir Alec Douglas-Home (Prime Minister 1963–4), and Leon Brittan (Home Secretary 1983–5) had been made to look *shifty* by television. "It's a cruel medium," he said, and several other speakers in the same radio programme referred to Mr Brittan's "rather unfortunate public personality" as conveyed by television.

Elsewhere Alan Watkins has pointed to another implication for politicians of living in the television age: the effect on their repertoires of such unremitting exposure to the medium. A nineteenth-century voter would gladly walk a round trip of ten miles or more in order to hear Mr Gladstone speak once in his lifetime.

Gladstone could, therefore, make substantially the same speech (or as Aneurin Bevan did, sixty years later, tell the same joke) many times over. But modern politicians have to develop different material, as well as a variety of appropriate styles, for recurrent appearances before the same mass audience.

The lessons learned by politicians from their unrelenting exposure on television have not been lost on professionals in other walks of life who recognize the need to develop the full potential of their public personalities, and especially their voices. This has led to the creation of services like that described by a *Daily Telegraph* article in April 1987. An actress and two drama teachers have set up an organization which, for a fee of around £20 an hour, offers to "align voice with ego". "Salesmen, senior management, businessmen, and more and more working women who have problems with pronunciation" – this means, in effect, accent – "shyness, public speaking, mumbling, or just making themselves heard" are seeking out their service. And, along with middle-managers from Citroën and salesmen from Nissan, are the aspiring politicians.

The political implications of the television age have their worrying side, with the emphasis on the packaging rather than the real political content, the medium rather than the message itself. Against these dangers must be set the reflection attributed to the novelist Sir Compton Mackenzie, who speculated that had television started earlier it might have prevented the rise of Hitler and Mussolini, whose achievement of power in democratic states would have been thwarted by the close scrutiny of their real nature which this all-too-revealing medium offers.

Another consequence of the emergence of television in politics is that the accents of political figures have become a much more crucial ingredient of their public personalities, and it is not surprising to hear claims that Harold Wilson, John F. Kennedy, and Margaret Thatcher all adapted their accents in the course of their political lives. The accent which Kennedy's advisers told him he would have to modify if he was to win the presidential election in 1960 was the Boston hyperlect, the American equivalent of the poshest form of British (marked) RP. That Kennedy should have acquired this accent in the first place was due to the determination of his parents to break into the exclusive Boston 'aristocracy' which, despite the great wealth and social prestige of the Kennedy family, had never really accepted them. Kennedy's efforts to tone down his hyperlectal accent were sufficiently successful for him to gain the presidency. Of around seven front-runners who competed with Walter Mondale in 1984 for the Democratic nomination to stand against Reagan later that year, age and other personal factors were regarded at an early stage as likely to rule out the chances of several of them. In the case of Senator Fritz Hollings of South Carolina it was his voice. A British commentator wrote that the Senator "is nimble witted and looks the part, but speaks in such a rich southern accent that his TV commercials have to have a 'voice over'." Jimmy Carter's mild version of the Georgia accent was apparently regarded as within the bounds of intelligibility, and it did not stop him winning the presidency in 1976.

Margaret Thatcher is a classic example of an individual's rise from humble origins through merit, determination, and effort. Her parents both came from working-class backgrounds: by sheer hard work and sound business sense – qualities her supporters would claim she has inherited – they achieved success in running a modest grocer's shop in Grantham, Lincolnshire, and Margaret and her elder sister Muriel grew up in their house above the shop. It has been said that after winning a scholarship at the age of ten, which took her from the local state school to the town's grammar school for girls, Margaret took elocution lessons. If this is true, it must be noted that such lessons were common for girls in that type of school at that period, along with music and other accomplishments. Even so, biographers stress that after she won her way to Oxford to study for a degree in chemistry, she arrived there "an unsophisticated lower-middle-class Lincolnshire girl". She was later quoted as saying of her Oxford days, "When I got there, I think the first thing I learned was that, for the first time in your life, you are totally divorced from your background."

It may have been at Oxford, therefore, that she adapted her accent to the rather posh, marked RP variety which was detectable when she was first an MP (from 1959) and then a Cabinet minister (1970). After she replaced Edward Heath as leader of the Conservative party in 1975 – and reputedly with a great deal of help from her adviser Gordon (now Sir Gordon) Reece and from the Conservatives' highly successful public relations agents Saatchi and Saatchi – she went to some trouble to modify her hairstyle, and, even more, the pitch of her voice, replacing its hint of stridency with a more soothing, persuasive quality. It may be that her accent's hyperlectal features also became less obvious. In 1982 dental problems required that a number of her teeth be capped, which slightly changed her enunciation.

A year before Mrs Thatcher became Prime Minister, the historian and socialist writer A. J. P. Taylor, after watching her on television, reassured his wife that the leader of the Conservative party was in no danger of achieving power "as she has such an awful voice". Three spectacular and, indeed, historic election victories have exposed the fatuity of such forecasts. But despite, or even because of, the changes urged by her advisers, her voice and speaking manner are still controversial in Britain. In its 1965 guise her "impeccable" accent was said to be "like some Roedean water torture"; the *Observer's* political correspondent Adam Raphael wrote in 1985 of "her hectoring schoolmarm approach", and Conservative reverses in Scotland in the 1987 general election led the editor of the *Sunday Times*, Andrew Neil, to observe on television that the Scots regarded Mrs Thatcher as "southern suburban". But most of her supporters in Britain would claim that her voice and accent give an impression of courage, authority, and decisiveness. In western Europe, political leaders appear to regard her, if not with affection, at least with great respect, and the Russians call her the Iron Lady. Americans are reported to be "fascinated" by Mrs Thatcher and by "the fact that she uses the English language with such a flourish". Though British journalists routinely use terms such as 'bossy', 'schoolmarmy', and 'shrill' of Mrs Thatcher's speaking manner, the writer Beryl Bainbridge has shrewdly observed that Mrs Thatcher had to make her way in a man's world, where women have to shout to be heard.

It is not only Conservative politicians from humble backgrounds who modify and re-modify their accents. Harold Wilson grew up in Huddersfield and in Cheshire, and won his way to Oxford where in 1939 he became a don. By the time he was a very young President of the Board of Trade under Attlee in the 1940s he had an accent very close to RP, but on becoming leader of the Labour party in 1963 (and Prime Minister in 1964) his accent began to re-emphasize the northern vowels of his boyhood, perhaps consciously as part of the image he strove to promote of the 'common man', never appearing in television interviews without his pipe.

When Neil Kinnock succeeded Michael Foot as the Labour party's leader in 1983, he had no need for the kind of 'vowel surgery' apparently resorted to by Harold Wilson, Margaret Thatcher, and John F. Kennedy. Mr Kinnock has the perfect accent for a leader of the Labour party. It is close to RP, but has just enough Welshness, of the more educated sort, to give reassurance that he is not identifiable with the Establishment in Britain, or even with the upper middle classes. He is also a remarkably fluent — sometimes, indeed, torrential — speaker. Some would say that it was entirely because of these vocal gifts that Mr Kinnock was chosen as party leader, since he had no experience of holding office in any previous Labour government, and was chosen over the heads of dozens of colleagues who did have such experience, in some cases substantially so.

The choice of Neil Kinnock conforms to the pattern described at the beginning of this chapter, where the ability to project a public personality which shows up well on the media may become the crucial qualification for political leadership in advanced societies in a television age. His supporters would claim that his talents amount to more than just this, and that his campaign to rid his party of left-wing extremists reveals a forcefulness of character which, despite his complete inexperience of government, augurs well for his future chances of becoming Prime Minister. Despite political differences I react favourably to Mr Kinnock's voice and accent. I love its slight Welshness and musicality. Only rarely is intelligibility at risk: when he said at a Westminster rally in October 1985 on Aid for the Third World (reported on BBC TV news):"The need is no greater than it has been before", his *no* was meant to be RP's *now*, implying a completely different meaning. Purists find fault with some of his linguistic usages, such as his confusion of *infer* and *imply*, and his occasional lapse into a minor linguistic quirk called 'metathesis', the transposing of sounds in a word. On his election as party leader, he used in more than one of his speeches the word 'em-nity'(enmity).

The contemporary politician who has, because of his accent, suffered most from the new requirement for political figures to satisfy the prejudices of a national television audience is Roy Jenkins, who became a peer in 1987. Product of a humble Welsh grammar school, Jenkins won his way to Balliol College, Oxford, and later, as a Labour politician, he held, with some distinction, two of the major offices of state, becoming Home Secretary and Chancellor of the Exchequer. On his return to Britain after serving as President of the European Commission, he was the most eminent of the Gang of Four Labour politicians who broke away to form the Social Democratic party, and he was briefly its first leader. Yet Roy Jenkins's credibility and influence as a national political leader – indeed, even his ability to win and hold on to a parliamentary seat as representative of a minority party – were crucially compromised in the 1980s by one aspect of his public personality, his accent. In the transition from Welsh grammar school to Balliol, Jenkins moved not just towards RP but over the top, into the marked form which would have been totally appropriate in the 1930s and 1940s to a future Cabinet minister, but which the democratization of accents would render unacceptable thirty years later in the new world of maximum radio and television exposure. It was an adaptation which would not even have been helpful in that later period to a future Conservative politician, of the kind more common at Balliol, whose Oxford experience (according to an *Observer* article on Michael Foot's contemporaries there) involved "locking oneself into the lavatories at Balliol and emerging with a plum in one's mouth." (More than twenty years later the future Labour politician Bryan Gould arrived as a Rhodes Scholar from New Zealand to study law at Balliol. "On his first day he took the voices he heard outside his room to be deliberate caricatures.")

Roy Jenkins's hyperlectal accent has the typical feature which gives *cawst* for *cost*; when he very nearly won the Warrington by-election for the new SDP in 1982 he declared to the nation on the radio, "Though we *lawst* this election, we won a great victory . . ." There is the use of the impersonal pronoun: "factors such as how *one* has slept . . ." (ITN, 1982); when elected Chancellor of Oxford University in 1987 he said on a BBC Radio 4 programme, "I got a very good education at Oxford which has been, I think, the bedrock of *one's* life."

The feature of his accent that has been the subject of the most explicit comment in the media is his handling of the letter *r*: it was even used in a *Times* cartoon involving Jenkins and the new SDP in 1983. In it Jenkins was proclaiming the slogan, "Incwease gwowth and weduce VAT." This way* of pronouncing *r* is not

* Not to be confused with the distinctive and very different Northumberland *r*, which was commented upon as early as the 1730s by Daniel Defoe. "I must not quit Northumberland without taking notice that the natives of this county . . . are distinguished by a shibboleth upon their tongues, namely, a difficulty in pronouncing the letter *r*, which they cannot deliver from their tongues without a hollow jarring in the throat . . ." This 'uvular' (or 'gargled') *r* can still be heard in rural Northumberland, but is not a characteristic of Newcastle Geordie.

restricted to any social class; it is more often a personal idiosy-cracy, though its prevalence among some members of the upper classes has a long history.

In the nineteenth century Disraeli commented on this feature among several of his contemporary MPs, and on its tendency to limit the effectiveness of their speeches. One long-serving member of the Commons told him, "I have observed no man in this House can have success, who can't sound his *r*s." But two very considerable parliamentary speakers in the twentieth century have given the lie to Disraeli's informant. Aneurin Bevan, Minister of Health in 1945 and architect of the National Health Service, was in his time reckoned to be the best speaker in the House of Commons after Churchill himself, and this despite both a stammer and the same sort of *r* trouble as Roy Jenkins. Brian Walden, who went up from a grammar school in West Bromwich to The Queen's College, Oxford, was probably the most brilliant platform orator to enter public life in the post-war period, though his parliamentary career later fizzled out and he lost his socialist beliefs. As presenter of a TV current affairs programme he has had less scope to display the oratorical brilli-ance which triumphed over his Jenkinsian difficulty with the letter *r*. So it is not the sound of *r* itself which was Roy Jenkins's downfall, but its combination with all the other hyperlectal features which made the *r* sound the last straw. When he stepped down as leader of the SDP in 1983 a national daily newspaper explained his relative lack of success as leader by saying that he "lacked the common touch", a delicate way of referring to his accent. A more recent judgement on his public career, by *Sunday Times* columnist Edward Pearce, was more brutal. He described Jenkins as "a man who spent a lifetime trying to cast off the shame of working-class connections, strangling innocent vowels and lisping like a Castilian nobleman."

There must be lessons for us to learn from the tragic waste of talent involved in this story. Mr Jenkins was a victim of the fact that the rules changed twice during his lifetime – the rules about which accents were acceptable in public figures, and the rules about how much a politician's own personal characteristics became public property through close scrutiny on the new media. After all, before 1922, the year of the foundation of the BBC radio service, and the year in which Roy Jenkins reached the age of two, a politician's voice would not be heard by more than 7 per cent of the population throughout his entire lifetime. There were direct consequences for British political history in these personal events. If Roy Jenkins's national image had enabled him to impose and retain his authority on the SDP, the split in that party would probably never have happened. Did nobody ever tell him what was so incongruous about that image? Was he too proud to change or to seek help? Did he feel it was too vital a part of his identity by then? Or would it have been too late anyway – would the media and voting public have allowed the necessary changes to pass without comment and without reacting with even more pointed forms of ridicule?

The natural place to expect to find this very posh form of accent among politicians is, of course, in the Conservative party. What few people have noticed is how little represented this accent actually is among Tory MPs, even among the Conservative top brass. If Mrs Thatcher has herself lost the traces she once went to some trouble to acquire, her predecessor, Edward Heath, never had them. Neither his years at Balliol nor his sensitive musical ear induced him to overdo the adaptation to RP from the accent of the very lower-middle-class Broadstairs background in which he grew up. Indeed, his accent has retained several of those original features, which continue to be satirized in *Private Eye*, and during his premiership in the early 1970s a hostile recording of his voice, artificially emphasizing his southeastern vowels, was made and circulated by some of his upperclass critics in the Conservative party.

By contrast, long-serving Tory MP Julian Amery has been a classic example of the hyperlect and of the way the organs of articulation were pre-set in order to produce some of its most distinctive sounds. What Amery could not be taken as an example of, however, is another specific characteristic of some speakers of marked RP, which is better represented by certain other Tory MPs, several peers, and many men and women among the landed gentry and the professions. This is the tendency for speakers with the marked RP accent to be able to utter sentences that are ungrammatical or clearly lacking in logic, and to get away with this because the social prestige of the hyperlect diverts attention away from the questionable grammaticality, or the patent illogicality, of what they are saying. It may be that unmarked RP speakers are also given the benefit of the doubt in this respect because their accent is associated with authority and competence, whereas the same faults would appear to be magnified when spoken in a non-standard accent. This is a subject crying out for serious empirical research.

Many prominent Conservative politicians nowadays speak not pure RP, but a paralect of RP. Both Norman Tebbit and Norman Fowler have minute traces of the 'popular' London accent, Tebbit's being a very close paralect, Fowler's a broader one with more easily identifiable London elements. Former Conservative Cabinet minister Enoch Powell has slight Birmingham features, though not as broad a Birmingham paralect as that of morals campaigner Mary Whitehouse. Kenneth Clarke's paralect has minute traces of his Nottinghamshire upbringing, though certainly not enough of them to justify the second half of a description in a *Times* profile: "Clarke has never deserted his Midlands base, *or his accent.*" John McGregor, Agriculture Minister in 1987, has that most acceptable of all paralects of RP, the one with slight traces of the educated Scottish accent. All of these – together with the straight RP accents of other Tories of humble origins like John Moore and Cecil Parkinson – are much more suggestive of real bonds with the common people than the accents of privileged public-school products in the Labour party like Michael Foot and Tony Wedgwood Benn. This is even more true of the Rt Hon. Sir Rhodes Boyson, who proudly proclaims his regional origins by his Lancashire accent. This did not prevent him from becoming one of the most successful state school headmasters in Britain, an effective government minister in several departments, and one of the most sought-after speakers to Conservative audiences all over the country.

More striking still is the number of new Conservative MPs, especially since 1983, with accents much more obviously down-market than any we have so far discussed. This has been a matter of comment from several quarters. From journalist and Conservative MP Julian Critchley (Shrewsbury School and Oxford):

> As Mrs Thatcher has gone up in the world, so the party has gone down. In the last twenty years the old officer class, which provided the ballast in the House [of Commons] has steadily given way to the 'new men', the entrepreneurs, the Rotarians, the estate agents, the small-town solicitors, and most important of all, the professional politicians who have climbed the ladder of opportunity, let down, in the guise of the Young Conservatives, into the tennis-playing suburbs by Lord Woolton and others.

Critchley went on to refer to "The Round Tablers, and the tax advisers, publicists and brokers who have inherited the safe seats, once the preserve of the double-barrelled . . ." Writing elsewhere on the same theme, Critchley was more explicit about the implications of such backgrounds in the way the 'new men' in parliament speak: "small town solicitors and estate agents with *flat provincial accents*".

From the public school men who run *Private Eye* there was a comment in similar vein in the 'Dear Bill' series of spoof letters purporting to be from Denis Thatcher in 10 Downing Street to an old golfing crony. This referred to the character of Tory representation in the Commons following the swing to the party in the 1983 general election:"The place has filled up with the most grisly detritus of common little oiks ever seen on the Tory back benches." Earlier, *Private Eye* had named three Conservatives as "graceless new-boy MPs": in fact they all have non-standard accents. Another Tory MP of 'the class of 1983', a personnel consultant who once taught in a primary school in Bethnal Green, has a non-standard accent which includes the *-in* for *-ing* feature characteristic of the most 'popular' London speech. Patrick McLaughlin, elected as Conservative MP for West Derbyshire in the 1986 by-election and again in the 1987 general election, has the kind of accent one would expect from a former miner.

The claim of the Conservative party to be the party of the people – in striking contrast to its upper-class image of earlier generations – can only be strengthened by such a range of accents, though old-fashioned journalists from Labour party backgrounds may find them hard to accept. Thus Alan Watkins in the *Observer* on the Newcastle-under-Lyme by-election in 1982, in which the Conservatives fielded a candidate born in Wolverhampton: "He talks in an unaffected Midlands accent. He is clearly a perfectly nice man. But he is equally clearly just not up to it. His difficulties with the English language are not so great as those experienced by the new Conservative Member for West Derbyshire, but they are getting on that way."

Again, what is at issue is not the possession by a public figure of a non-standard accent, but *which* non-standard accent it is, and its degree of breadth. Sir Cyril Smith, Liberal MP for Rochdale, has a Lancashire accent rather broader than Sir Rhodes Boyson's, but there is never any threat to his intelligibility, and his accent is an essential part of his public image. So it was, too with the late David Penhaligon, the very able Liberal MP for Truro until his tragic death in a road accident in 1986, who wore his Cornish accent like a badge. It was a crucial element in his enormous popularity among people of all parties (though there was at least one listener to be found who complained of Penhaligon's appearance on a BBC Radio 2 programme: "His speech delivery was terrible"), and there is no reason to disbelieve David Steel's claim in June 1987 that he had earlier marked out Penhaligon to succeed him as leader of the Liberal party. His delivery was, in fact, clear and confident, ringing with the competent yet unthreatening rusticity of the Westcountryman.

A commentator in the *Financial Times* claimed that Penhaligon's accent became even richer on the radio: "You can almost smell the apples and hear the cows in the background", and this despite his never having lived on a farm, and his frankly confessed ignorance of matters rural. So powerful was this association of ideas generated by his accent that soon after he became an MP he was baffled to find himself much in demand to be interviewed on the media about the Common Agricultural Policy and other farming matters. (The same kind of association of ideas is exploited by television commercials for Norfolk turkeys, which emphasize the East Anglian pronunciation 'bootiful'.) Beside Penhaligon, his fellow-Liberal and former MP for a Cornish seat, Paul Tyler (public school and Oxford) has an impeccable but colourless RP, which seemed to make a mockery of his protestation on a BBC Radio 4 *Any Questions?* programme in 1984, "I'm very proud of coming from Cornwall."

Commenting on the fact that Conservative candidates in Scotland did badly in the 1987 general election, the historian Professor Norman Stone said, "I do not believe that the Conservative cause will ever recover. The Conservatives speak with foreign accents and have different ways." This is a strange judgement if it is meant to apply to MPs, especially in comparison with Scottish MPs of other parties, several of whom sound very English, including Michael Bruce, a Liberal MP who speaks pure RP, and former Labour MP Robert Maclellan, elected leader of the pro-merger SDP in 1987, whose close RP paralect has barely detectable Scots traces. And then, of course, there is Tam Dalyell . . .

When, many years before his death in 1987, the twelfth Marquess of Huntly, premier marquess of Scotland, observed of the members of the House of Commons that they "had hardly an *h* between them", he was presumed to be referring to the non-standard accents of Labour MPs. Yet Labour governments since 1945 have always contained a generous proportion of RP speakers, including public school and Oxbridge products like Attlee, Cripps, Crossman, Crosland, Wedgwood Benn, and Jay. For about a quarter of a century the Scottish constituency of West Lothian (now Linlithgow) has been represented by the irrepressible Labour MP, Tam Dalyell, whose accent and other vocal features make his voice virtually indistinguishable on the radio from that of a long-serving Tory Lord Chancellor, Lord Hailsham. This is not really surprising since both went to Eton (many years apart) and to aristocratic Oxbridge colleges (Dalyell to King's, Cambridge, Hailsham to Christ Church, Oxford). Labour's Shadow Education Secretary from 1984 to 1987, Giles Radice, whose accent is the product of Winchester and Oxford, struck commentators as incongruous if he had to speak for his party in Commons debates on subjects such as trade unions, even though he had once worked for one. There is no doubt that a public school background may have become a disadvantage to an aspiring Labour MP in recent years. In 1979 Christopher Catherwood, son of the industrialist Sir Fred Catherwood, who won the Cambridgeshire constituency in the elections for the European Parliament, was reported as having "defected from the Labour camp, claiming that he was discriminated against because of his public school accent". The former public schoolboy who fought and won the 1986 Fulham by-election earned this description from the *Observer*: "A Reptonian, his voice has the 'classlessness' of the politically ambitious public schoolboy of the 1960s."

The stereotypical Labour MP is Dennis Skinner, who sits for the Midlands seat of Bolsover. We are not allowed to forget that Mr Skinner once worked as a miner: the journalist Margaret van Hattem refers to Skinner's "gravelly Derbyshire accent and ability to make standard English sound like dialect". Yet Mr Skinner had the privilege of a grammar school education and attended Ruskin College, a trade union college loosely associated with Oxford University. His present accent is clearly part of his political message, and in his *Who's Who* entry he insists on reminding us that he comes from "good working-class mining stock". Yet such an image would serve him ill if he became a Cabinet minister and had to use television to influence public opinion nationally. Here a paralect like Dr John Cunningham's (with slight traces of Jarrow) or Bryan Gould's (whose minute New Zealand traces put him beyond the labels of the British class system) would serve him better; Labour front-bencher John Smith's more full-blooded accent is acceptable because it is educated Scottish (heaven help him if it were broad Glaswegian) but he will have to be careful it is not perceived in England as too threatening in its nationalism.

Larry Whitty, who became general secretary of the Labour party in 1985, was educated at a direct-grant school and at Cambridge. "His flat-vowelled London accent and sober style of dress", as a Sunday newspaper profile reported, "make him appear classless – no handicap in a very class-conscious movement." But a wider spectrum of accents is to be heard at an annual Labour party conference. The Blackpool conference of the party in 1984 worried Alan Watkins:

> My most abiding recollection of Blackpool is of the violence of the language, to which the *rude and menacing accents of Glasgow and Liverpool*, disproportionately evident throughout the week, are especially suited.

It is among the trade union element in the Labour party that non-standard accents are, if not compulsory, at least a valuable asset. When Ron Todd became the general secretary of a major union, the Transport and General Workers', in 1985, at the age of fifty-eight, the *Observer* wrote this of him:

> A smart but not flashy dresser, with an unreconstructed Cockney

accent bearing the imprint of his native Walthamstow in East London, he could easily be mistaken for an off-duty market trader.

Norman Willis became general secretary of the Trades Union Congress in 1984. On leaving school in Kent he was employed by a trade union (the Transport and General) and went up through Ruskin College and on to do a degree at Oriel College, Oxford. Any trace of adaptation towards RP in his Oxford days has been reversed since he became a leading trade unionist, and never more so than when his criticism of the miners' strike threw into question his solidarity with parts of the union movement. Indeed, the need to emphasize 'popular' London features in his accent extended into the use of non-standard grammar. Television viewers who saw extracts of his address to the TUC conference at Blackpool in 1985 heard him saying, "Of course, we don't never get those problems because we're always right."

Arthur Scargill, leader of the Yorkshire miners and president of the National Union of Miners, is one man whose commitment to the class struggle can never for a moment be in doubt. This certainty enables him to adjust his accent to suit his audience. When interviewed on national TV – as frequently happened during the long miners' strike of 1984–5 in which he played a key role – he used an accent so close to RP that he even dropped the characteristic northern *u* in words like *industrial*. But on the platform at a northern miners' gala, he could switch back to a full northern *u* sound in the first syllable of his "Courage, comrades!" This flexibility, provided it involves authentic-sounding versions of the accents used, can be a real strength in a political figure, and must be counted part of Mr Scargill's skill as a communicator, whatever we may think of his ideological stance. But, for all his general language abilities, his use of body language is all wrong: his gestures are frequently ill-timed and distracting.

Roy Hattersley, who became deputy leader of the Labour party in 1983, has none of these accent problems. His accent is close to RP, with enough of Sheffield left in his voice to authenticate his regional and class origins. But he has two faults which have the power to distract, and thus weaken his effectiveness as a communicator. One of these he shares with another politician, Dr David Owen, the rest of whose accent and speaking manner are a major element of the attractiveness that once led large numbers of voters to support him and the undivided SDP of which he was leader. At least two other voices regularly heard on the media also have this peculiarity, Alan Whicker and Sir Robin Day. This is the allocation of unnatural emphasis to the indefinite and definite articles, so that 'a' (normally unstressed, as in *a dog*) and 'the' (as in *the dog*) come out as *ay* and *thee*. So we have, from Mr Hattersley, "*a* independent nuclear weapon" and "*a* uncle", on the BBC *Any Questions?* radio programme; and "*a* internal party analysis" (BBC *World at One*): and, from Dr Owen, "*a* open society"; and from all of these media speakers we are likely to hear talk of *thee* government, *thee* media, etc., the form normally used only before a vowel (as in th*e* end). All this is part of an increasingly common tendency among media speakers to exaggerate the importance and sense of urgency of what they say by allocating extra stress in various abnormal ways.

A second potential source of distraction and annoyance among listeners to Mr Hattersley is a personal idiosyncrasy. By an extension of the increasingly common treatment of *a* and th*e*, which we have just discussed, there is an arbitrary, pedantic and altogether excessive allocation of emphasis to more words or syllables in the sentence than usually receive such treatment. In Mr Hattersley it results in an explosive issue of words, which initially attracts attention but eventually becomes a matter of irritation – not necessarily at the *content* of what he is saying, since Mr Hattersley often has important and interesting things to say.

But we cannot expect all politicians to be perfect. If they were all careful models of elocution, as actors used to be expected to be, it would become very boring. Indeed, despite Ronald Reagan's success in the USA, actors as a class do not often succeed in politics, and certainly not on the quality of their diction alone. Of the actor chosen to contest the Darlington by-election for the SDP in 1983 a political columnist wrote, "He has a beard and a nice voice, though it is an actor's voice, made deeper than it is naturally, and with the words over-carefully enunciated." The candidate went on to do badly in the vote and afterwards withdrew from politics.

Those who regard it as a matter of concern for the political integrity of democratic societies that the quality of media presentation appears to have become more influential on the electors than the actual ideologies and policies of the candidates, will have taken comfort from the British general election of 1987. In this campaign Neil Kinnock and the Labour party out-Saatchi'd Mrs Thatcher. Mr Kinnock was reported as having undergone a minor operation a few weeks before the election in order to remove from his head a tiny bump that advisers feared might somehow impair his public image. His party spent millions on party political broadcasts, some of which were, by common consent, of an exceptional quality, so good indeed that, within months, extracts of Mr Kinnock's own contributions were plagiarized by Senator Joe Biden, one of the candidates in the race for the Democratic nomination for the 1988 US presidential election. Yet Mr Kinnock and the Labour party, who had seemed within reach of victory, suffered a crushing defeat. So perhaps there are grounds for hope that the electorate is now becoming more sophisticated and politically mature, in being able to see behind the faces, the hairdos, the accents, and the real or imagined bumps on the head.

EIGHT

Changing patterns

It is still common in Britain for job advertisements to specify 'well-spokenness', which implies clarity of articulation and a restricted range of accents which certainly excludes any broad regional or social accents. To quote from a random selection, a restaurant manager is sought who "should be well-spoken, of smart appearance, and highly efficient" (*The Times*, 1984). A sales executive (with good sales experience) is wanted: "well-dressed, well-spoken and with an easy manner" (*Daily Telegraph*, 1985). An administrative assistant for a barristers' chambers in London WC1 "must be well-spoken" (*The Times*, 1987). Not only managers, administrators, and executives need this quality, but also the secretaries who work for them and often stand between them and the public. Advertisements like the following are not untypical: "The General Manager of a successful and expanding company dealing in specialized marine insurance is looking for a well-spoken senior secretary (60 words per minute) . . ." It goes on to make clear that duties include dealing with a constant stream of visitors (*The Times*, 'Super Secretaries' column, 1983). A *Times* advertisement in 1985 for a boy to play the film role of a seventeen-year-old specified only one quality besides gender and approximate age: "Perfect standard of English". Few potential applicants would interpret this as other than a reference to a standard accent. When the contributor of an article in *The Times* in 1985 on 'the inarticulate voice of youth' implied that unattractive accents were partly responsible for the high totals of unemployment among young people, a correspondent wrote in suggesting that mass unemployment had killed off the ambition which in the past had motivated the young to adapt to more acceptable accents.

A real difficulty for all young people today is that such confusing messages are reaching them about the implications of accents. For example, how inseparable is accent from educatedness? On the one hand there is the long history of high-profile people adapting to RP in the course of extended education. On the other hand there are the exceptions to this, and the protestations of those who claim that such adaptation is treachery to one's origins and one's 'real' identity.

The Oxford scholar A. L. Rowse has often told the story of how, as a boy of nine from a barely literate home background before 1914, he resolved to speak differently from the local lads in his elementary school in Cornwall. The historian A. J. P. Taylor's patriarchal grandfather, born in 1848, "spoke broad Lancashire – the full dialect, not merely an accent, with lovely words now almost forgotten such as *oo* (for she), *gradely*, and *baggin*." His father, with a grammar school education, took over the family's prosperous cotton business: he spoke "pure northern English, though he could speak broad Lancashire as well."

"I began with a Lancashire accent," writes Taylor, "and lost it at Oxford, much to my regret. I can hardly speak real Lancashire now though I can understand it, and my sons tell me I develop an accent as we go north." He went in 1919 to Bootham, a Quaker boarding school in York which at that time barely enjoyed public school status, and when he went up to Oxford he still had "no manners and a rough Lancashire accent". This accent he "unintentionally" lost during his undergraduate days at Oriel College where social life, as in most Oxford colleges in that period, was "entirely dominated by the products of public schools".

The writer Anthony Burgess grew up in much humbler

circumstances in Manchester. "My grandfather spoke a modified form of the Lancashire rural dialect, one suitable for the outskirts of a great city. I inherited the accent, if not the vocabulary, and had to work hard to lose it." He explains one of the reasons for doing this: "It was not taken seriously outside Lancashire. London saw it or heard it as a wilful and comic deformation of Received Standard, suitable for George Formby Senior or Junior but to be despised as a medium for serious discourse." When he joined the army as a recruit to the RAMC, Burgess found that, surrounded by illiterate fellow-rankers and unintelligible Glasgow NCOs, his accent "grew unprecedentedly posh: I declared war on the bastards."

For those who, on going up to Oxford, adapted their accents – but only to a limited extent, doggedly retaining a number of features which proclaimed their regional origins – there might be a price to pay. The historian Alan Bullock was one of the great figures of post-war Oxford and virtual creator of the modern St Catherine's College. As Lord Bullock his name was mentioned early on as a possible candidate for the chancellorship of the university in 1987, but a newspaper report speculating on the field for the election said that, "He makes rather too much of his Yorkshire accent for some of senior Oxford's taste." One college head was quoted as saying, "There is a slightly utility quality about him. He is a good, durable garment, but made of somewhat inexpensive material." Many distinguished academics do, like Lord Bullock, retain strong traces of the non-standard accent with which they grew up – unless, of course, it is one of the most disfavoured ones – while moving *towards* RP but not as close as would constitute a paralect. But, if their accent does travel only thus far, this is often made the subject of comment about them. Thus *The Times* obituary of Sir Norman Chester, who rose to become warden of Nuffield College, Oxford, refers to his working-class origins, and then to his establishing himself as a don at Oxford around 1949: "He was steadily adapting himself to his new surroundings, becoming more donnish and

less spruce, while retaining his Northern directness and Lancashire accent." Some of the same accent was retained throughout
his life by the notable economic historian T. S. Ashton, a
professor at Manchester University, according to his entry in the
Dictionary of National Biography.

After taking part in discussions on some of my judgements
about the way accent works in contemporary Britain, a friend
of mine who teaches at a polytechnic in the North of England
was sufficiently interested to set down for me an account of his
personal experience of these competing pressures. He has
allowed me to quote from it at length:

> As a boy at a local authority grammar school in the mid-1950s, in
> a semi-rural mining area in north Derbyshire, I became conscious
> around the age of thirteen to fifteen that most of the academically
> inclined boys and girls (the latter, particularly) were changing
> from the local accent (something between that of Sheffield, on the
> one hand, and Derby on the other, but to a sensitive ear quite
> distinctive) to a 'Received' pronunciation. I myself felt a strong
> ambivalence about it all: a strong desire to advance my own
> academic education as much as possible, which obviously meant
> going to university, and on the other hand, a wish to retain
> solidarity with my own home area and social class of origin, as I
> perceived it. I struggled, therefore, to keep my accent as intact as
> possible – there was no explicit attempt by the school to influence
> pupils in this respect – while resisting (politely, I hope) suggestions
> from the school that I try for Oxford. I applied to northern
> provincial universities, obtaining a place at Manchester.
>
> Whilst at university I hung on as much as possible to my
> local accent (not so very different from that at Manchester) and
> encountered resistance only in half-friendly jibes from friends
> there who came from more middle-class backgrounds, who
> claimed that retention of a northern accent would impede career
> prospects. One instanced his uncle, a Lancashire librarian, whose
> promotion, he claimed, had been impeded by his Lancashire
> accent.
>
> When I did a postgraduate teacher-training course at Man-
> chester University, I was one of a group singled out at the

beginning of the year to be offered 'Speech Training', but the classes were optional and I certainly did not go, once I discovered that the aim was to train us in RP. My unwillingness seemed to be accepted by the university department.

From then on, I encountered little comment. I taught in my local area for five years, was then appointed to a full-time post with a teachers' union by a committee consisting of a Welshman and a Geordie, and, in the late 1960s, after three other interviews, I obtained a post at a teacher-training college. Interestingly, it was at this stage that well-meaning advice was offered to me by fellow-employees. One senior teachers' union official – a southerner – advised me that I would need to modify my accent to obtain a local government post in educational administration, and at an interview for a teacher-training college post in Herefordshire, an older candidate being interviewed on the same afternoon for a different post advised me that, the way he had sized it up, a northern accent would be a disadvantage at this particular college. (He recommended Australia as being a country where the possession of a British regional accent would not be a bar!)

At the same time as my friend was bracing himself to withstand all these pressures, thereby asserting what he felt strongly to be an important fact about his identity, there were, as we have already seen, pressures operating, for some, in the opposite direction. Young people of privileged education went to great lengths to disembarrass themselves of RP accents and, as Alan Watkins commented in the 1970s, "young women of gentle birth and lengthy education" (he gave as examples Labour MP, Harriet Harman and Labour parliamentary candidate, Patricia Hewitt) "took to screaming at the top of their voices, 'Comreyds . . . we want Sowcialism neow.' " It was presumably a similar generation of products from certain educational institutions that a *Times* TV critic had in mind when he referred to a television discussion featuring a psychologist whom he described as having "a faint Cockney accent, which seems obligatory now in all the caring professions". The producer of a successful television series was quoted in 1983 as saying, "I have found that some younger teachers in the inner city areas deliberately adopt a slovenly way of speaking in order to communicate more freely with their pupils." And then there is the anguish of the Hon. Paul Foot, son of a peer and colonial governor, beneficiary of an elite education at Shrewsbury School and Oxford, who has taken up the 'hard left' version of socialism represented by the Socialist Workers' Party, and who bared his soul on the BBC's *Any Questions?* radio programme: "I've been fighting against my accent all my life. I've tried to forget about it. I wake up in the night, remember it – it's a bit of a nightmare."

Recognition that accents such as RP can cut people off from those with whom they wish to identify is exemplified by a Scottish duke, educated at Eton and Oxford and a speaker of unmarked RP, who told me he had deliberately chosen not to send his son to his old school, but rather to a public school in Scotland, in order that his son's accent should not create a barrier between himself and the staff who worked on the landed estate he would inherit. (He also told me the idea had not succeeded: many products of Scottish public schools speak RP, as indeed do most of their teachers.) Peter Bowles, the actor best known for his performance as the parvenu squire in the TV series *To the Manor Born*, went at the age of sixteen to the Royal Academy of Dramatic Art from Nottingham and worked hard to lose his regional accent at a time just before the 'new era' when regional accents became more acceptable on the stage. He now claims to regret the loss of his regional accent – "the essence of my identity had been interfered with" – and for a time his self-confidence suffered. Whether he could have secured the roles which brought him his TV success without having adapted to RP must be regarded as extremely doubtful; in any case many actors manage to retain their original accents while adding others to their repertoire. Michael Caine, who, like Albert Finney, is often cited as an example of an actor who created a new tradition of acceptability for (very slight) non-standard accents in theatre, television, and films, rationalizes it differently.

Since working as an actor in the USA, where he finds that 'plummy' English and authentic regional accents are incomprehensible to most movie-goers, Caine has deliberately ditched the Cockney accent with which he grew up. His latest films show him using a very close paralect of RP. According to an interviewer, "Caine is contemptuous of English actors who boast of their integrity and refuse to dilute an accent to make their English more recognizable."

An ITV documentary series on the lives of a group of children filmed at seven-year intervals since they were aged seven showed the process of identification working in both directions. The lives of fourteen children born in 1956 and from very different backgrounds in Britain were filmed first in 1963 ('Seven Up') and at intervals thereafter. The episodes screened in 1984, when the subjects were by now aged twenty-eight, showed how a very bright little seven-year-old boy with a strong Yorkshire accent had won his way to Oxford, had brain-drained to America and was now a physicist at the University of Wisconsin: his accent had moved very noticeably towards RP. But the very posh accent displayed by several of the others as young children had also been modified. One, in particular, was a boy who had been to a preparatory school, to the public school St Paul's, and to Oxford to read mathematics. After experience as a missionary and in insurance he was now shown teaching mathematics and computing in a multiracial school in the East End of London. His accent had lost all traces of the hyperlect of his boyhood.

The ideal answer to the individual's dilemma about changing his accent – 'upwards' or 'downwards' – is code-switching: the ability to move between two or more accents (or dialects) which enables the speaker to show his sense of community variously with the educated speakers of RP or with groups who express their regional or class identity by a non-standard accent. We have already seen this at work in Arthur Scargill. Though most people have some ability to do this, in relation to at least one accent besides their normal one, the distribution of this skill in the population, the number of accents an individual is likely to be able to attempt, and the range of characteristic accent features that he or she is likely to be able to reproduce authentically, are limited. Notwithstanding the Arthur Scargills, Mike Yarwoods, and Jim Davidsons, code-switching is full of pitfalls. The worst of them is that speakers of one variety who attempt another which, it becomes obvious, is not their own – either because they don't get it completely right, or because they are clearly very high-status figures attempting a low-status accent – are invariably regarded as being patronizing. Informants have told me of at least two cases of headmasters – in one case of a grammar school, in the other an independent school – each of whom grew up among speakers of a strong local accent. On revisiting his native heath each prides himself on switching into the local accent in (say) the local pub. Instead of welcoming this reassertion of solidarity and shared values, the local people are reported to resent it as somehow belittling them.

Denis Healey, elder statesman of the Labour party, speaks an RP paralect with slight traces of his Bradford boyhood, and can clearly switch with confidence into a more robust Yorkshire accent, what we learned earlier to call a mesolect. But during the 1983 general election campaign the *Observer* columnist Simon Hoggart followed him around the Midlands constituency of Walsall. "Mr Healey found a group of young men hanging about. 'Wotcher, boys,' he said heartily. He always gives the impression that he learned his slang from a Berlitz course; somehow it's not quite right." A notorious victim in recent times was Peter Tatchell, who stood as Labour candidate for the Bermondsey seat in south-east London in the 1983 by-election. His upset defeat by a Liberal owed much to his left-wing associations and, even more, to unpleasant smears by a section of the press concerning his tolerant attitude to homosexuality. Another contributory factor was certainly his unfortunate, though well-intentioned, attempt at code-switching. His own accent is 'educated Australian', but BBC 2 television coverage showed him canvassing around Bermondsey in a fair imitation of an East End accent. (Both accents had a common local ancestor but have moved apart in the past 150 years!) Several people commented adversely on this to me, letters to the press made the same point, and in his assessment of the by-election result in the *Sunday Telegraph*, Ivan Rowan said that Tatchell *patronized* the voters of Bermondsey, "and for that he was not forgiven".

Some thirty years ago the English writer and socialist J. B. Priestley, whose broadcasting voice was known to millions of BBC listeners, wrote a piece in which he argued that, far from indicating moral worth, the readiness to change an accent could well indicate a propensity to dishonesty in other areas of life. A man who will cheat himself out of the speech of his boyhood may not hesitate, he claimed, to swindle the shareholders or humbug the electorate. But Priestley, who had a privileged university education at Cambridge, himself spoke with traces of an educated Yorkshire accent, nothing like the basilectal 'ee bah goom' variety. Moreover, he was certainly ready to pass scathing comments on certain other regional accents – for example, that of Tyneside, which he claimed to find "barbarous, monotonous and irritating", and "equally objectionable" in the mouths of men or of women.

If we consider Britain's 'black' population (a term about which I am uncomfortable, but it will serve in this context), i.e. British residents mostly of Asian or Afro-Caribbean descent, we see that the use of one accent rather than another poses dilemmas in relation to the group with which they thus express their identity. In general, there is a high correlation between adaptation to British accents (though not necessarily of course to RP) and commitment to, and integration into, the British way of life. In the case of West Indians, there is a high correlation, among teenagers, between the conscious adoption in adolescence of a West Indian accent (and often of other features of the patois such as its grammar) and under-achievement in school. As is also the case with vernacular Black English in the USA, the adoption of such speech forms often goes hand in hand with hostility to education, with blatant forms of sexism, and with forms of discrimination against those follow black pupils who co-operate with the school and resist pressures to steal, smoke, take drugs, and indulge in other forms of criminality. A sharply contrasting example is that of the Black Pentecostalist pastor, originally from Antigua, shown on a religious programme from Nottingham on BBC television in 1984. Both he and a young black man who gave a testimony during the service had accents very close to RP. They are both involved in running Saturday classes in the city for young West Indians whose educational ambitions are frustrated by forms of discrimination which they feel operate against them in the official school system. Their reaction is to show young West Indians how to break into that system by exploiting the standard form of language and accent in Britain.

But there are plenty of others to be seen, on television programmes for blacks and by blacks, making comments implying that only by talking Black English can a black person in Britain assert his identity and self-respect. A newspaper feature in 1983 on a girl brought up in Britain who went back to Jamaica to rediscover her origins showed, on her return, that she had changed her name from Barbara to an African name, had adopted an Afro hairstyle, and that her public school accent had become heavily Jamaican. There are plenty of people with an ideological interest in – and often a career to be made from – promoting the notion of 'alienation', and opposing adaptation to recognizably English speech forms and the assimilation which this facilitates. That racial prejudice, often in very nasty forms, is an obstacle to such assimilation is almost too obvious to be stated: the question is, which strategy is most likely to challenge it successfully? One relevant pointer is the evaluation experiment in the USA which showed that the voices of black speakers using standard accents were rated more favourably than those of white speakers with non-standard accents. Similarly, tests have shown that the voices of black children born and bred in Cardiff cannot be identified as black by white listeners. Further evidence comes from the success of black representatives on the British media.

The television newsreader Trevor McDonald (who has an RP accent with occasional paralectal features deriving from the West Indies) and the comedian Lenny Henry (with traces of an English Midlands accent) may have done more to counteract irrational prejudices against blacks in Britain than two decades of commissions, inquiries, and reports. There is also a large supporting cast of other television presenters, reporters, and actors whose names and faces indicate membership of ethnic minorities but whose RP accents defuse much of the prejudice, distraction, and possible unintelligibility which their media contributions might otherwise generate.

Politicians, too, have now got the message. Any member of an ethnic minority who wishes to have his voice heard outside his immediate community is likely to move towards an RP accent. This is true of all three of the 'representatives' of the immigrant community who were invited on to a BBC *Panorama* television programme in 1981 to discuss the Brixton riots: Councillor Russell Profitt, Paul Boateng, and Rudi Narayan. Of these, Paul Boateng, whose background is Anglo-Ghanaian, and who became an MP in 1987, has several features of the marked variety of RP. These hyperlectal features are only slightly less apparent in another MP elected in 1987, Keith Vaz, from an Asian background but educated in Cambridge. The third of the black MPs elected in 1987 was Diane Abbott, MP for Hackney, who went to grammar school and Cambridge, where she "developed what she describes as a hatred of the 'British ruling class' but caught its accent" (according to an *Observer* profile). Only the fourth of the quartet of black MPs elected in 1987 has any trace of a non-standard accent. Bernie Grant came to Britain soon after completing his schooling at the hands of the Jesuits in Guyana. Nearly a quarter of a century later his accent still carries a dash of the attractive flavour of the Caribbean. Now

MP for Tottenham, he proclaims that "Black people are beginning to break through into the areas of influence" in Britain.

At a much more mundane level, a lecturer colleague married to an Asian lady reports that his dark-skinned son was, with two other such lads, stopped by a policeman one night in a Midlands city. The policeman's accusatory manner changed noticeably when the lecturer's son replied in a polite RP accent. An Asian family saved from deportation from Britain by the determined support given them by their (mostly white) neighbours on the private housing estate where they lived, were shown by television coverage to speak with an accent close to RP. Such signals of identification with the wider community in Britain have considerable power to defuse the hostility of the host population. Another reminder of the association of RP with social acceptability across racial barriers was given in one of the numerous radio programmes in the early 1980s which fed the widespread public nostalgia about India in the days of the British Raj. An Indian contributor whose privileged origins were advertised by an accent very close to marked RP – and very different from the normal Indian English accent – recalled how in the 1930s as a young man he had installed himself in a first-class railway compartment on an Indian train on which he had a reservation. A British army officer wishing to use the compartment came in and started shouting angrily that this offensive 'object' of an Indian must be removed. On being addressed politely by the young man with an accent possibly more hyperlectal than his own he immediately changed his tone, and with effusive charm invited the young Indian to share his compartment.

After a rebellious adolescence, the son of Rhodesian Premier Ian Smith took up religion and wrote a book about his change of heart on a number of issues, including African nationalism. In it he describes how, in the absence during the civil war of any real information on the state-controlled media about the African nationalist leader Mr Mugabe, who was dubbed 'The Red

Terror', the white population were surprised when they were given their first chance to see and hear him. "When he appeared that first night on television to announce the independence of Zimbabwe to the nation, many whites were taken off guard by this *cultured, well-spoken* and *highly articulate* man who was now their prime minister." (My italics.) The contrast may have been the more striking in that Ian Smith's own accent contained the *-in* for *-ing* pronunciation, which in his case was certainly not an aspect of the marked variety of RP.

It would, of course, be ridiculous to claim that merely by adapting to RP the members of ethnic minorities would conquer all the forms of adverse discrimination, of both subtle and blatant kinds, which beset them in Britain. Nor could it be claimed that speakers of the most disfavoured accents would, by the fact of adaptation to RP alone, triumph over all the social inequalities which still remain in British society. But the crucial fact is that adaptation towards RP is, rightly or wrongly, perceived as a signal of an individual's identification with the values of the wider society, and especially with such notions as educatedness and competence. Non-standard accents signal narrower loyalties, to a region, a class, or even to a set of religious beliefs or to a group sharing a particular outlook and lifestyle. For, just as Catholics and Protestants in Northern Ireland use certain pronunciation features to tell each other apart, so some Catholics on the English mainland cultivate special pronunciations of particular words which constitute shibboleths (I have heard Catholic priests do this with the nouns *convert* and *confessor* (CUNvert and CONfessor), and many Catholics – and Anglo-Catholics – have a distinctive pronunciation of the word *mass*, rhyming it with RP's grass, and use a similar long *a* in *Catholic*). In London there is a sub-variety of Jewish accent, and both in London and some other big cities of the English-speaking world there is a distinctive accent among male homosexuals.

The long-standing taboos on the public discussion of accents and their implications, and on the confrontation of these issues in our schools, have been maintained by people at opposite ends of the ideological spectrum. On the one hand there are conservative-minded people who do not want to open up to scrutiny and possible criticism the class system of which accent variety is seen as an integral part. On the other hand there are the egalitarians, including many linguistic theorists, who shrink from drawing people's attention to facts which have the potential to humiliate non-standard speakers, and who claim that, far from attempting to alter the disfavoured accents of members of certain groups, classes or regions, we should bend our efforts to *changing national attitudes* to accents. The method to be used to achieve this is, curiously, that of suppressing all serious public discussion of the reasons why such prejudices persist, and by simply promoting the principle of tolerance of linguistic diversity.

It is extremely doubtful whether this latter tactic will succeed, in our own lifetime or indeed our children's, and I will offer two reasons why I think this is so. First, the hierarchy of accent prejudice in Britain has, as I have shown, a long history, and long-established social attitudes have a resilience which we would do well to recognize. It is true that in the past thirty years attitudes on such subjects as illegitimacy, premarital sex, and homosexuality have been transformed – indeed on two of them the pendulum is swinging back again. But all of these issues were a matter of intense public discussion and debate and changes were part of a pattern of complex social forces. Even if we defy the taboo and open the subject of accent up to informed debate, it could take fifty years or more before there are any signs of change. Meanwhile millions of children will suffer from the present widespread ignorance about the subject. (It is also true that fifty years from now the extremes of accent variation will have narrowed still further, by a continuing process of natural attrition which has more to do with the influence of the media than with explicit campaigns for linguistic tolerance.) Secondly, and more importantly, I believe that the reaction to accents in Britain is a mixture of irrational prejudice, defensible value judgements, and rationality, and those rational and defensible elements, when opened up to public discussion, may actually serve to increase the pace at which individuals move away from some non-standard accents towards the standard. We must return to this theme in our final chapter.

NINE

Accents and the future

In the past two decades the world has witnessed an explosion in the demand for the English language. In addition to some 300 million native speakers (mainly in Britain, the USA, and Britain's 'Old Dominions') there are about a billion people around the globe who speak English as a second language at least in some basic sense. This accounts for *one in four* of the entire population of the earth, constituting both a total and a proportion which are without precedent in the history of the human race.

There is, of course, a price to pay for this explosion. Every year some less widely spoken languages die, and many others find their vocabulary swamped by English words, and even their grammar, word order and idiom adjusted in imitation of English.

The vast majority of foreign learners of English choose between two models, American English and British English. According to an American professor of English linguistics writing in 1980, "until recently there was no doubt that standard English from the international point of view was the British variety", but the cultural prestige of British English as a model for foreign learners is offset by the economic and political power and influence of American English, and the two models now seem to be in fairly equal competition in educational systems around the world.

A second important factor is that, despite the differences in pronunciation between American and British English, it remains the case that, in general, a speaker of the standard form of either variety can understand, and be understood by, other such speakers in any part of the world. The *non*-standard varieties of both British and American English are, however, a different matter. So are the heavily indigenized forms like Indian English and West African English. Twenty years ago it must have looked as though the indigenization of English, as it came to be spoken by more and more people in countries where it was taught by teachers whose pronunciation of it was influenced by a heavy overlay of the local language, would inevitably escalate to the point where English would fragment into hundreds of varieties whose speakers would be barely comprehensible to each other, as has already happened in some parts of the world.

Fortunately the means now exist whereby this process can be halted and, given enough determination, reversed. We have seen how the mass media of the spoken word have, in recent years, come to exercise a powerful role in advanced societies, and their linguistic influence is one of standardization, rather than differentiation or indigenization. Similar standardizing tendencies are beginning to be seen in developing countries, and it is at least possible that speakers of English in those nations will in future have available not only films and television programmes as models of American and British English, but also an array of video and other teaching aids which will give learners ready access to sophisticated instructional programmes using teachers who speak an international variety of English. All this will be going on in a context in which the new technology of the communications revolution and the information revolution are saturating all the countries of the world with material spoken in a standard variety of English.

The world-wide tendency, then, must be towards greater standardization and uniformity of English. (This leads on, of course, to the further question of how far the pronunciation of British English and American English can ultimately be kept apart.)

There are additional reasons why greater uniformity is desirable and indeed inevitable. International communication in areas of high risk such as air traffic control and marine navigation is already conducted in English. A number of major air accidents have already been attributed to the failure of air traffic controllers or aircraft pilots to use sufficiently standardized and comprehensible English. Other disasters include demolition explosions which have gone wrong because of imperfect communication among speakers of different varieties of English, or imperfect speakers of a standard variety. All point to the need to move towards a greater uniformity of pronunciation world-wide.

The closer we move to the year 2000, the more obvious it becomes that our own and our children's lives, if we live in advanced countries, will be made easier by a proliferation of gadgetry in the home, the car, the factory, the office, and the shop, which will perform automatically many procedures previously requiring human effort. Already some of these automated procedures involve giving out instructions or warnings in a recorded human voice that the toast is ready, the car radiator needs topping up or the tyres need more air, the photocopier needs to be fed more paper, or that today is your wedding anniversary and you should remember to take flowers home. Some of the most expensively engineered German cars now have voices giving out appropriate warnings in seven languages, two of these 'languages' being English pronounced respectively with an American and a British (RP) accent.

Machines are increasingly designed to respond to instructions from the human voice. But clearly it will not be practicable for the most advanced forms of robotic machinery either to make announcements, or receive instructions, in more than a very small number of languages or a very limited number of varieties of the accents of one language.

For many years the industry of teaching English as a foreign language has been sensitive to the need to teach a standard accent. In effect, this has meant either British RP or General

American. Recently, voices have been raised claiming that, for British English at least, this is a form of snobbery, and that foreign students should be brought closer to the common people by being taught a vernacular accent or a regional accent like Yorkshire. Whether a Japanese businessman or a Brazilian physicist would thank you for teaching him such a variety is more than doubtful: what, most of all, the foreign learner is likely to want is a standard accent with all its connotations of educatedness. (In any case, RP is probably more widely intelligible throughout the British Isles than any other variety of accent.) In practice, the demand for teachers of English world-wide is such that many of them have accents which reflect the whole spectrum of variation. They include mother-tongue speakers with strong regional accents and others who have learned English as a foreign language and show this clearly in the way they speak it. The use of teaching materials which employ either RP or General American as their model helps to counteract the effects of this, and increasingly in the future a wealth of audio and video resources will be used to help the learner acquire the standard accent.

In Britain and many other countries, especially in Western Europe, job advertisements for teachers of English to foreigners frequently make veiled references to the desired accent. Some are more frank, stating specifications such as: "Qualifications and experience not essential: energy, appearance and accent more important." Advertising in *The Times*, a German girl of eighteen wanting to improve her English by staying with a British family specified a home "where the Queen's English is spoken", and a Japanese school of English advertising in Britain for a teacher requested a "well spoken lady". In Singapore, the official policy of the Ministry of Education is quite explicit. Recognizing that this tiny nation's economic future is crucially connected to its citizens' ability to communicate internationally, it has set out to reverse the relative degree of indigenization that has produced 'Singlish' (Singapore English). Advertisements in the British educational press in January 1988 for teachers for schools in Singapore required that they be speakers of "the Queen's English".

Our acceptance of the need for increasing standardization of English pronunciation in the face of all these international and technological realities must not blind us to the fact that the standardization we are talking about is relative. Nobody is pretending that within the next fifty years the entire population of Britain will, or ought to, change to speaking a version of RP so standardized that robot machines will not require to be programmed to cope with a degree of breadth of accent in the voices to which they respond. Even RP in its purest, textbook form is not so completely standardized as to have only one correct pronunciation for every single word. Consider the following list of words which we hear almost every day of our lives: *been, ate, room, year, often, again.* Each of these can be pronounced in two different ways by educated speakers of standard British English. The same is true of the phrase *police constable.* (One syllable for *police* is increasingly common among speakers of both marked and unmarked RP, and the first syllable of *constable* has two pronunciations in unmarked RP.) There is a whole set of words which contain the syllable *or* or *ar*, about whose pronunciation there is no clear agreement among RP speakers: *secretary, temporary, regulatory, primarily, ordinarily;* and *terrorist* and *deteriorate* also cause uncertainty. The *i* in words like *finance, dilemma, direct* can be pronounced in two different ways, as can the *ss* in *issue* and *tissue* (and the central *t* in *initiate*), and the *e* in *economics* and at the beginning of *envelope.* Choosing between the two options for *schism* has been known to cause schism, and there are two words which all speakers of RP seem to find virtually unpronounceable: *veterinary* and *dioceses.*

These examples show that a fraction of 1 per cent of the total vocabulary of an educated speaker of British English allows of more than one pronunciation, which, of course, is not impossible for a computerized robot to handle. But in principle there is a good case for accepting the logic of standardization and agreeing, wherever possible, on a single pronunciation for every word, though the attempt to do so for a word like *controversy* has so far always provoked controversy. There would be merit, too, in agreeing to tinker with the pronunciation of those words which give rise to frequent misunderstandings. *Aural* used sometimes to be pronounced like *oral*, since many words like *authority* and *audience* had established that pronunciation of *au*, but the confusion between what relates to the mouth (oral) and to the ear (aural) has led to a change in the pronunciation of the first syllable of *aural* to make it sound like *our*. The more frequent incidence of terrorist acts has made it more urgent that we try to distinguish between the verbs *defuse* and *diffuse*, since defusing tension and diffusing it mean opposite things, a point frequently overlooked by newsreaders. There is a similar case for restricting the pronunciation of the prefix *non-* in *non-smoker* and *non-violent* to *non* rather than *nun* (as some say it), because *nun* already means something else, whereas *non* is nowadays used by RP speakers only as a prefix. A more controversial proposal is that we should try to pronounce the numerals thirteen to nineteen differently, or else to pronounce the tens from thirty to ninety in some other way (e.g. giving the final *-ty* the sound of *tie* in *necktie*), since international communication – and the safety of millions who rely on the precise understanding of messages exchanged over the airwaves – depends on a crystal-clear distinction between these numbers, in ways which our medieval forebears could not have foreseen when the English numeral system evolved.

Standardization can provide these benefits, but it also involves loss. The richly diverse linguistic forms of the historic dialects and 'basilectal' accents are a precious part of our heritage – like the blacksmith, the village stocks and the ducking-stool, and a thousand other historic artefacts and customs from our past. Their loss is part of the price we pay for modernization. Sentimentalists like me mourn their passing with a special grief because unusual linguistic phenomena are as fascinating to a student of language as butterflies to a collector, or exotic fertility rites to an anthropologist.

A practical disadvantage attending the reduction of accent differences over the next fifty years will be a decreasing reliance on accent features to identify wrongdoers. At present, police descriptions of wanted criminals often mention a specific local accent (or, in other cases, 'well-spokenness' which, not surprisingly, is frequently an attribute of confidence tricksters) which can sometimes be a readier means of identification than height, build, or hair colour. Many police forces throughout Britain retain the services of specialists in accent and dialect who can give important information on the recorded voices of, say, people who make hoax telephone calls to fire brigades. Occasionally such procedures misfire, as when the hunt for the Yorkshire Ripper was unduly extended – and more lives were lost – because attention was diverted away from the real culprit after a cruel hoaxer with a north-eastern accent made a number of telephone calls to the police claiming to be the Ripper.

When Charles Glass, an American journalist kidnapped by extremists in the Lebanon and forced at gunpoint to make a propaganda video for them, eventually escaped his captors in 1987, he revealed that in the video he had used an American Southern accent to try to indicate that he was being held in the southern suburbs of Beirut. Whether the right people got this message is not clear, but such strategies depend on the existence of accent variations which are certain to reduce, in the USA as in Britain, in the face of pressures towards standardization over the coming century.

So from one point of view the English-speaking world is set to become a duller place. Though I will not be alive to witness the new, grey world in which the old regional and social accents are reduced to mere traces of their former richness, the ones I would miss most would be those which have become my favourites, usually because of happy memories of living and working, in my formative years, in places where they are spoken: Cockney, Scouse, Lancashire, Edinburgh Scottish, and – sweetest of all upon my ear – Newcastle Geordie, with its distinctive grammar and vocabulary as well as the music of its spoken form.

What reconciles me to the gradual and eventual passing of accent varieties in Britain is my awareness that accent differences are one of the greatest obstacles to genuine social equality in this country. So long as accents persist, they will be made the excuse for some people to discriminate against others and belittle them. It is no accident that the USA, where a much larger proportion of the population speak with a standard accent (General American) than is the case with RP in Britain, is plausibly regarded as a much more open and genuinely democratic society than our own. A similar judgement has been made on Australia, where nearly everybody speaks with the same accent, though in a varying degree of breadth.

There is a simplistic argument which says that rather than requiring the child to adapt to society, we should change society to accommodate the characteristics of the child. Those who use this argument to deny children access to any awareness of the implications of speaking with one accent rather than another are doing them an obvious disservice, if they cannot also guarantee that society's attitudes will have changed in time for that generation of children to benefit. Sadly, such a guarantee is impossible, if only because, as I have repeatedly stressed, accent involves a more complex set of judgements than mere social snobbery.

A few years ago I was invited to take part in a programme on a local radio station, in which, along with another professor, I discussed the significance of accents with two groups of teenagers, one from a south-east London comprehensive and the other from a public school. One fourteen-year-old black girl expressed, in very vehement terms, her disbelief that her very strong Cockney accent could ever entail any kind of prejudice or disadvantage to her in life: she had already discovered that she could go down into the neighbouring London borough and find plenty of young people who spoke as she did and accepted her as one of themselves. My professorial colleague urged her equally strongly to disregard anyone who might suggest that the ability to speak only in this one accent could carry any disadvantage. Though I was not given an opportunity to say so, I could think of many situations in which this strong local accent would limit her chances in life, certainly if she stepped outside the boundaries of her local community and its immediate vicinity. It was ironic that the advice was given her by a professor who had himself made the transition from a local London accent to the RP without which he would have been very unlikely to have secured his professorship. Moreover, he had chosen a neighbourhood in which to live, and schools for his children to attend, which ensured that they too did not have to go through life speaking as he was encouraging this young teenager to persist in doing.

What is really at issue here is a child's right to an 'open future'. By discouraging that girl from expanding her repertoire of accents to include a standard one, we are determining in advance the kind of opportunities of work, social contacts, and lifestyle generally she will be able to enjoy. The presuppositions of Shaw's *Pygmalion* in 1912 were echoed in a *News Chronicle* article in 1956 by two journalists, E. Arnot Robinson and Jill Craigie: "If you were a good fairy, hovering over the cradle of an English child today, the most prized gift you could bestow on it would be an impeccable accent." They were echoed again in 1983 by the Cockney comedian Jim Davidson, himself the master of several accents, when interviewed on the *Wogan* programme on BBC1 TV. He explained that he wanted to secure a "posh" education for his young son, partly because of the quality of the teaching the boy would receive, and partly because of the "correct" accent he would acquire.

The genuine 'openness' of any child's future is bound to be compromised by possession of a strong non-standard accent, since such accents are themselves the characteristic of a closed rather than an open system. The Cockney child, the West Indian child, the Glaswegian child or, for that matter, even the Eskimo child, is able to acquire a standard English accent because it is formally taught: there are teachers, teaching materials, and a mass of other access points in society which will facilitate the process of learning or adapting to the standard. But the Cockney, Glaswegian, or West Indian accent is a closed system: outsiders cannot learn it formally and it can only be acquired by the chance factor of having been brought up in a relatively enclosed community. Moreover, its speakers often use it to advertise their rejection of many of the values of the wider society – such as educatedness and social mobility – and to assert their localism, their particularism, their in-group system of values which is designed to exclude outsiders like you and me. At one level the persistence of local accents is merely a quaint and harmless survival from the past, but at a more serious level it is an expression of a form of tribalism, the type of society dominated by kinship or other such arbitrary networks which cause a person to be valued because he is a member of a specific group rather than for any merit or competence he may display in the duties society requires of him, and where status is ascribed rather than achieved. The RP accent is sometimes alleged to make its speakers sound threatening, but it is no less true that individuals can be subjected to powerful forms of intimidation at the hands of local communities whose social cohesiveness is symbolized by a particular regional or class accent.

I believe too, that well-spokenness is an attribute of human dignity, and that we owe it to all children to make it readily available to everyone. It is true that well-spokenness is, in part, a social construct – that is, like so many aspects of the use of language, what counts as well-spokenness is heavily determined by generalized value judgements which reflect social pressures. I also recognize that well-spokenness is closely related to the value ascribed to certain formal and literary uses of speech, a fact which makes it difficult for speakers of certain low-prestige social accents like Cockney, Birmingham and Scouse to be adjudged well-spoken because of the limited repertoires of those accents in relation to formal and poetic usage. But if speakers of certain localized forms of English find it difficult to gain acceptance for their accents as vehicles for elegance and precision of language, they have a right to be pointed in the direction of the standard accent – or, indeed, any accent of English which is regarded as appropriate for those uses – and to be given every facility in acquiring it.

Well-spokenness may be a crucial ingredient of an individual's self-respect. Christine Keeler was a society call-girl whose involvement with a Cabinet minister led to his resignation in 1963 and rocked the Conservative government of Harold Macmillan to its foundations. Twenty years later she discussed with the *Observer's* Simon Hoggart the ghost-written 'auto-biography' published that year under her name. Though she acknowledged that the book had, as she said, "got me right", there was one word in it she did not like, for it said that she " 'was just a pretty scrubber . . .' I wanted them to change it to *tart*. Scrubber implies someone who can't talk properly, and wears horrible clothes, but *I always spoke well*, and had good clothes . . ."

Whether we like it or not, the ability to handle one of the most widely acceptable accents has become an important indicator of an individual's ability to control the world around him. As such, it is a signal which must prove of great interest to an employer, and we know that accents play a significant role in influencing the often crucial first impressions formed at job interviews. Yet none of this area of human behaviour is opened up for discussion to children in schools. As we have seen, Britain's teachers have for decades avoided the subject, and their conspiracy of silence has in many schools been compounded by a reluctance to offer children an opportunity to celebrate and imitate examples of 'good' spoken English. The important Kingman Committee set up by reforming minister Kenneth Baker to advise on how English should be taught produced its much-heralded Report in March 1988. Its handling of spoken English was perhaps its weakest aspect: it completely funked the complex issue of accents, and even managed to get its facts wrong in its passing reference to the origins of RP.

The new 16-plus examination system, which started in 1988, with its provision for the assessment of oral English, may furnish some opportunities to remedy this lack. But a far more direct and pervasive consciousness of the implications of accent must be built in to much earlier stages of children's schooling. The first step must be to develop a more informed attitude among teachers, so that they may learn to handle with greater confidence this highly sensitive topic, in which children have to come to realize why their and their parents' perfectly 'normal' speech forms may expose them to unfavourable reactions outside their immediate social group, and ultimately limit some of their own options in life. All this argues for the study of language in all its working parts – grammar included – to be restored to a place in the schools from which it has so often been missing for two decades or more, with untold consequences for the linguistic insecurity of the mass of the population. At the same time it has to be squarely recognized that any return to the old practice which relied on shaming pupils for their non-standard accents can only do more harm than good. The required delicacy presupposes great skills in the teacher, though not necessarily more than those involved in teaching the issues surrounding social class to lower-class children in O level (or GCSE) social history or sociology.

When the taboo on the discussion of accents in schools is finally lifted, what shall we tell them?

All children in Britain should have it explained to them that accents are widely judged as not being of equal worth; instead there is a hierarchy in which some accents are very highly rated because of their perceived associations with educatedness and competence. Certain other accents are disfavoured for a number of reasons, some of them arbitrary (like associations with industrial conurbations rather than with the fragrant countryside) and some more understandable, like the absence of any recent history of literary or poetic speaking styles, or any associations with educatedness generally. Positive qualities sometimes attributed to the most disparaged accents are compassion and good humour.

They should be told that in England the most highly regarded accent is the unmarked RP of the stereotypical BBC newsreader, but that in Scotland and Northern Ireland, and to some extent in Wales, the educated accent of the region competes with RP for top place and in some contexts may be perceived as preferable. The most educated Scottish, Northern Irish, and Welsh accents are highly acceptable in Britain generally, though when any significant degree of breadth of such accent is used outside the region concerned there is a danger of unintelligibility, or at least of distraction from the speaker's message, *and even of actual hostility* (as some broadcasters have found).

This factor of breadth affects all non-standard accents in Britain. The most widely acceptable form of any non-standard accent is that form (the paralect) which is closest to RP, while retaining tiny traces of the original accent, and in circumstances where sociability or humour are the essential qualities, this accent is likely to be more serviceable to the speaker than RP. The marked form of RP (the hyperlect), which was once of great advantage to the social standing of its speakers, is now regarded as incongruous other than among members of the royal family, and should thus be avoided.

Speakers with non-standard accents should be encouraged to widen their repertoire to include unmarked RP (or a paralect); there are situations in which the ability to speak a non-standard accent in addition to RP could be useful, to a minister of religion or a social worker for example, but such speakers should be aware of the danger of being perceived as patronizing when code-switching 'downwards' is attempted, especially by those who do not get it quite right.

Children should be warned to expect that in the real world their accents may be used as an indicator of their origins, the extent of their educatedness, the system of values with which they identify, and whether these are associated with a narrow local group or with the wider society. They should be told of the world-wide pressures towards linguistic standardization, and of the increasing weight which is likely to be put upon general linguistic competence as the technology of everyday life becomes ever more sophisticated. At the same time they should be advised that, while some will tell them that a good wine tastes the same when drunk from a crystal goblet or from a chipped cup, the English language is a treasure trove of precious things whose beauty can, at least in some degree, be measured in the way they are spoken.

Young people should have the chance to ponder the confession attributed to a post-Second-World-War Labour politician, that he found himself unable to take seriously anyone who spoke with what he called a "common voice"; and they should be made aware of the generalized evaluations which may cause statements uttered in certain accents to lose some of their authority, since this may become crucial to their exercise of their rights as citizens and consumers – for example in making an effective complaint. They should also know of the new dominant role in society and politics of the mass media of the spoken word, and of the fact that the most effective users of those media are people who have learned to conform to the rules of social acceptability of spoken language, in whatever ways those rules might be deemed to apply at any given time.

In helping children to come to terms with the fact that accents provide social information on which they will inevitably be judged, they must be given opportunities to listen to their own recorded voices on tape, and helped to appraise the reactions of others to their voices, since it is well established that many –

perhaps most – speakers with non-standard accents are unaware of how much their speech varies from the standard.

They should be told, too, that the *Pygmalion* story as recounted by Bernard Shaw is based on a crude over-simplification of the way accents can work in British society to transform people's social status. Making Eliza into a duchess (or her father into a Cabinet minister) as Shaw claimed was possible simply by changing their accents, is a nonsense. When people move into a completely different social circle they need to know not just how to speak acceptably but also what to say, and how to behave in accordance with the manners of the group. Nineteenth-century writers of books of etiquette recognized this when they offered conversation material on topics in history, politics and even field sports, which a duchess would hear discussed around her in addition to social gossip. That Eliza would also need to know *what* to say was conceded by Shaw when he gave her her most famous line ("Not bloody likely!") the whole effect of which lies in its being uttered in a socially inappropriate setting. But even this detail is not authentic, since a genuine lapse into Cockney would have been much more likely to have produced "No bleedin' fear!"

Where Shaw was unquestionably right, however, was in calling urgent attention to language as a subject that deserves to be studied and, in both its written and spoken forms, taught more systematically to schoolchildren. As a nation the British are still woefully backward in both areas. We spend disgracefully little on research on the academic discipline of linguistics, and in school sixth forms and universities the teaching of the English language rates a very poor second to the teaching of English literature. If there is any truth at all in the suggestion repeatedly made in this book, that children's chances in life are seriously influenced by the ways in which they handle language in its spoken form, and that a school-leaver's job opportunities, a newsreader's credibility, or a public figure's effectiveness as a communicator, are all affected by their accents, then we owe it to all these groups to institute regular evaluation experiments to update and extend our knowledge of exactly how these judgements apply to every variety of spoken English in Britain, and to identify the factors which might modify those judgements. Moreover, my suggestion that accent differences are progressively reducing, points to the need for the reality of the situation to be systematically monitored by properly conducted tests by specialists in linguistics. All these issues can only benefit by being brought out into the open. Only when they are given the means to *identify*, to *analyse*, and to *understand* the elements which help to make up the rich heritage of our spoken language will our children be fully able to cherish and celebrate it – and to use it to take more effective control of their own lives.

References

ONE: *What is an accent?*

p. 1 **Snobbery which brands the tongue:** A. H. Halsey, following George Orwell, *Times Higher Education Supplement*, 25th June 1982.

p. 1 **Two cultural nations:** Neal Ascherson, *Observer*, 6 April 1986.

p. 2 **Pygmalion (1912):** Act and page references in these notes are to the 1931 Constable edition, where the play is published alongside *Androcles and the Lion* and *Overruled*.

p. 2 **Flower-seller into a duchess:** I. 208; II. 216, 221.

p. 2 **Science of speech:** I. 207.

p. 2 **Other features characterize dialects:** see especially Michael Stubbs, *Educational Linguistics* (1986), 21.

p. 3 **Worrited:** V. 263; I. 207.

p. 3 **Lincolnshire dialect words:** G. Edward Campion, *Lincolnshire Dialects* (1976).

p. 3 **West Country dialect words:** see especially K. C. Phillipps, *West Country Words and Ways* (1976).

p. 3 **Them as pinched it:** III. 243.

p. 3 **The Doolittles' non-standard grammar:** see especially II. 233–4.

p. 4 **Devon grammar of 'to be':** this example is quoted from the school magazine *The Blundellian*, June 1881.

p. 6 **Five main categories of English around the world:** this over-simplified account should be supplemented by reference to Manfred Görlach's chapter, 'Varietas Delectat', in Graham Nixon and John Honey (eds.), *An Historic Tongue: studies in English linguistics in memory of Barbara Strang* (1988).

p. 9 **Good studies of varieties of English**: in addition to Görlach's illuminating classification, see Peter Trudgill and J. Hannah, *International English* (1982); R. W. Bailey and M. Görlach (eds.), *English as a World Language* (1982); and issues of the excellent international journal *English World-Wide*, now published in Holland by Benjamin's. On varieties of English accents, the incomparable authority is J. C. Wells, *Accents of English*, 3 vols (1982).

p. 10 **Len Deighton**: see, for example, his *Mexico Set* (1984).

p. 10 **Clive James**: *Falling Towards England* (1985).

p. 10 **Anthony Burgess**: *Little Wilson and Big God* (1987).

p. 10 **Accents hinder job prospects**: Liz Hodgkinson, *The Times*, 3 and 11 September 1985.

p. 11 **Two Scottish researchers**: R. K. S. Macaulay and G. D. Trevelyan, Report to Social Science Research Council of survey of language, education, and employment in Glasgow, and in a number of articles derived from that research, cited in the Preface to Macaulay and Trevelyan, *Language, Social Class and Education: a Glasgow study* (Edinburgh, 1977).

p. 11 **The English have no respect for their language**: *Pygmalion*, Preface, 195.

TWO: *Where did RP come from?*

p. 14 **How Shakespeare pronounced English**: the outstanding sources here are Helge Kökeritz, *Shakespeare's Pronunciation* (New Haven, 1953) and E. J. Dobson, *English Pronunciation 1500–1700* (2nd edn. 1968).

p. 15 **Correct pronunciation fostered and taught**: quoted from E. J. Dobson, 'Early Modern Standard English', in *Transactions of Philological Society* (1955), 25–54, also reprinted in R. Lass, *Approaches to English Historical Linguistics* (1969), 420.

p. 15 **Shires about London within 60 miles**: George Puttenham, *The Art of Poesie* (1589).

p. 16 **River Trent as boundary**: see Dobson (1955) and Lass (1969), 422.

p. 17 **Raleigh's Devon accent**: John Aubrey (b. 1626) claims to have learned this by talking with a judge who as a youth had known Raleigh. See Aubrey's *Brief Lives*, ed. A. Powell (Cresset, 1949), 324.

p. 17 **William of Malmesbury**: Cecily Clark, 'Another late 14th-century case of dialect awareness', *English Studies* (1981), 504–5.

p. 17 **Inferior, corrupt, hideous, or laughable**: Barbara Strang, *A History of English* (1970), 159–60.

p. 18 **Scottish English**: see especially A. J. Aitken, 'Scots and English in Scotland', ch. 30 of P. Trudgill (ed.), *Language in the British Isles* (1984).

p. 18 **300,000 English emigrants between 1630–90**: E. A. Wrigley and R. S. Schofield, *The Population History of England 1541–1871* (1981), 469.

p. 19 **Changes in the pronunciation of standard English 1600–1800**: a full scholarly account of these can be found in Strang (1970), ch. 2.

p. 20 **Comparative growth of London's population**: see articles by M. J. Daunton and by E. A. Wrigley in *Towns and Societies*, ed. P. Abrams and E. A. Wrigley (1978); and David Souden and D. Starkey, *This Land of England* (1985).

p. 21 **Proportion of French-speakers in France**: see especially Grace Neville, 'Minority languages in contemporary France', *Journal of Multilingual and Multicultural Development*, vol. 8 (1987).

p. 22 **Absurdity of Scottish or Irish elocutionists**: R. C. Bambas, *The English Language, its origins and history* (USA, 1980), 194.

p. 22 **Dr Johnson's accent**: C. Hibbert, *The Personal History of Samuel Johnson* (1971; Penguin 1984), 33, 197.

p. 23 **Mrs Montagu as friend of Johnson**: *ibid.*, 119, 260, 280–1, 291, 337. For Montagu's views on regional accents see J. Honey, 'Talking Proper', in G. Nixon and J. Honey (eds.) *An Historic Tongue* (1988).

p. 23 **Accent-consciousness of northern gentry**: Honey, 'Talking Proper' (1988).

p. 23 **Vicious pronunciation in Birmingham**: *ibid.*

p. 23 **Scottish accents in London**: J. Y. T. Greig (ed.), *Letters of David Hume* (1932), vol. 2, 148, 187. I owe this reference to Dr Margaret Bryant.

p. 24 **Lord Derby's Lancashire patois**: Disraeli, *Reminiscences*, ed. Helen and Marvin Swartz (1975), 93.

p. 24 **Prettiest little boy at Eton**: S. G. Checkland, *The Gladstones: a family biography* (1971), 138.

p. 24 **Peel's accent**: Disraeli (1975).

p. 25 **Proportion of boarders in nineteenth-century English schools:** John Roach, *A History of Secondary Education in England* (1986), 29, 126, 282.

p. 25 **Withdraw sons from local associations:** *ibid.*, 28–9.

p. 25 **Dr Thomas Arnold:** See T. W. Bamford, *The Rise of the Public Schools* (1967); and John Honey, *Tom Brown's Universe* (1977).

p. 26 **Infrastructure of preparatory schools:** D. P. Leinster-Mackay, *The Rise of the English Prep School* (1984).

p. 26 **"Where did you go to school?":** see especially Honey (1977), chs. 3 and 4.

p. 27 **Accents in nineteenth-century public schools:** Honey (1977), 231–3.

p. 28 **Network of public schools:** see Honey (1977), ch. 4, and John Honey, ch. 2 in B. Simon and I. Bradley (eds.), *The Victorian Public School* (1975).

p. 28 **RP at Oxford:** Honey (1977), 233.

p. 29 **Pressures towards RP in elementary schools:** Honey, 'Talking Proper' (1988).

p. 29 **Cockney's unpleasant twang:** *ibid.*

p. 30 **Local mobility over short distances:** D. Souden and D. Starkey, *This Land of England* (1985), 193.

p. 30 **Manual to correct Birmingham accents:** Honey, 'Talking Proper' (1988).

p. 30 footnote **Contamination by servants:** Ronald Fraser, *In Search of a Past* (1984), 13, 25–6, 83, 112.

p. 30 second footnote **England loses rural population:** This point has been frequently made in the writings of Oxford's history professor Norman Stone.

p. 31 **Evelyn Waugh, Lancing College incident, 1919:** see Michael Davie (ed.), *The Diaries of Evelyn Waugh* (1976), 31, 149–50; and Honey, 'Talking Proper' (1988).

p. 31 **Dirk Bogarde's wartime commission:** interview with Bogarde on *Omnibus*, BBC 1, 27 March 1983.

p. 31 **Accent tuition in Midlands grammar school:** D. J. P. Fink, *Queen Mary's School, Walsall* (1954), quoted in Honey, 'Talking Proper', (1988).

p. 31 **BBC on pronunciation:** see A. Lloyd James, *The Broadcast Word* (1935); and BBC, *Broadcast English* (1928; 3rd edn., 1935).

p. 33 **Sir Harold Acton:** *Observer*, 21 February 1982.

p. 34 **Prominent Anglican clergyman:** Honey (1977), 233.

p. 34 **Public School and University English, 1917:** *Times Educational Supplement*, 11 October 1917, 393. I owe this reference to Mr C. A. Stray of University College, Swansea.

p. 34 **Former apprentice from Saddleworth:** John Thornton, *Serious Warnings, addressed to Various Classes of Persons* (1830), quoted in Geoffrey Thornton, *Language, Ignorance and Education* (1986), 6.

p. 34 **Beatrice Webb:** *Diary of Beatrice Webb*, ed. Norman and Jeanne Mackenzie (1982), vol. I 1873–92, 324, 14 February 1890.

p. 35 **Period voice of East End Cockney:** C. H. Rolph, *Further Particulars* (1987), ch. I.

p. 35 **Sir William Robertson:** Honey, 'Talking Proper' (1988).

p. 36 **National servicemen surrounded by different accents:** article on national service by Brian Jackson in *Sunday Times* colour supplement, 28 September 1986; see also Trevor Royle, *The Best Years of their Lives: the national service experience 1945–63* (1986).

THREE: *Talking proper and talking posh*

p. 41 **'U' and 'non-U':** Alan S. C. Ross and Nancy Mitford, *Noblesse Oblige* (1956); see also Richard Buckle (ed.), *U and non-U Revisited* (1978).

p. 42 **Affected speech of courtly circle:** see Dobson (1955) and Lass (1969), 422.

p. 42 **Russian aristocracy use French:** see chapter on Russia by J. Blum in D. Spring (ed.), *European Landed Elites in the Nineteenth Century* (1977).

p. 43 **Second Earl of Sunderland:** for Sunderland (1640–1702), regarded as one of the "craftiest, most rapacious and most unscrupulous politicians of his age", see under Robert Spencer in *Dictionary of National Biography*. References to his accent and drawl are in the writings of the Hon. Roger North, notably his *Autobiography* and *Examen*. See A. Jessop, DD (ed.), *Lives of the Norths* (1890), especially vol. I, 303.

p. 43 **Centenarian's "cawfy":** man aged one hundred and three from Tunbridge Wells interviewed on BBC Radio on 21 June 1961. Information from BBC Sound Archives, January 1987.

p. 44 **Countess of Munster:** Honey, *Tom Brown's Universe* (1977), 236.

p. 44 **The impersonal 'one':** Dr K. C. Phillipps in his valuable *Language and Class in Victorian England* (1984), 76, shows how *Punch* ridiculed the excessive use of this form in 1844.

p. 44 **You was, it don't matter:** *ibid.*, 68–9.

p. 44 **Thomas Gray:** A. Attwater, *Pembroke College Cambridge: a short history* (1936), 98.

p. 44 **Harold Macmillan's 1981 interview:** Phillipps (1984), 69.

p. 44 **Sir John Gielgud:** interview on BBC Radio 4 programme on the dramatist and novelist Gordon Daviot, 13 November 1986.

p. 45 **Falklands Memorial Service:** excerpt on the *News*, BBC 1, 12 July 1982.

p. 45 **Hornby and Warre at Eton:** Honey (1977), 236.

p. 45 **Mrs Maud Yorke:** C. M. Bowra, *Memories 1898–1939* (1966), 164.

p. 46 **Aloof and pompous aristocrat:** the quotation is from Anthony Powell, *To Keep the Ball Rolling* (Penguin, 1983) Part I, 44–5.

p. 47 **Eton master's Yorkshire accent:** E. P. Rouse (Halifax Grammar School and Trinity College, Cambridge). See M. R. James, *Eton and King's* (1926), 60.

p. 47 **Accents and hierarchy in colonial Natal:** Tom Sharpe, *Riotous Assembly* (1971), 9 (my italics).

p. 48 **Mitford similarity in voice and feature:** Harold Acton, *Nancy Mitford* (1975), 9.

p. 48 **Accents of Deborah and Nancy Mitford:** BBC 2 programme on Nancy Mitford, May 1980; see also Jonathan and Catherine Guinness, *The House of Mitford* (1984); and Selina Hastings, *Nancy Mitford* (1985).

p. 49 **Universities as hotbeds of fashionable slang:** Morris Marples, *University Slang* (1950).

p. 49 **Oxford -er(s):** Honey (1977), 235.

p. 50 **If he can but learn it:** A. J. Ellis, *On Early English Pronunciation* (1869), 629.

FOUR: *Are some accents better than others?*

p. 51 **A standard textbook:** A. Hughes and P. Trudgill, *English Accents and Dialects* (1979).

p. 51 **Dr J. C. Wells:** *Accents of English*, 3 vols. (1982).

p. 51 **Half speak with some degree of northern accent:** *ibid.*, vol. 2, 349.

p. 52 **Welsh accents:** see especially Alan R. Thomas, 'Welsh English', in P. Trudgill (ed.), *Language in the British Isles* (1984), 178.

p. 52 **Rural Ulster dialects:** Peter Trudgill, *On Dialect* (1983), ch. 11.

p. 52 **West Indian language mixture:** this description is from Ashton Gibson, *The Unequal Struggle* (1986), 101ff.

p. 53 **Acrolect, mesolect, basilect:** these terms were originally established in the sociolinguistic description of language variation by two scholars working in North America, W. A. Stewart and D. Bickerton. See J. Honey, 'Acrolect and hyperlect, the redefinition of English RP', in *English Studies*, vol. 66, no. 3, June 1985, 247.

p. 53 **Elderly people with little education:** Trudgill (1983), 187.

p. 54 **Individuals' speech provides clues:** see especially H. Giles and K. R. Sherer (eds.), *Social Markers in Speech* (1979), Preface, xi.

p. 55 **Voice quality:** see especially John Laver, *The Phonetic Description of Voice Quality* (1980).

p. 55 **Liverpool adenoids:** D. Abercrombie, *Elements of General Phonetics* (1967), 94–5; also quoted in M. L. Samuels, *Linguistic Evolution* (1972), 19.

p. 55 **Lord Boothby:** obituary by W. F. Deedes in the *Daily Telegraph*, 18 July 1986 (my italics).

p. 56 **George Perry on Laughton:** *Sunday Times*, 6 September 1987.

p. 58 **Technique devised in Canada:** for a description and appraisal of the 'matched guise' technique developed by W. Lambert and colleagues, see especially H. Giles and P. Powesland, *Speech Style and Social Evaluation* (1975).

p. 58 **General picture that emerges:** see especially Giles and Powesland (1975). Other evaluation studies are cited in R. A. Hudson, *Sociolinguistics* (1980), including G. Smith (1979), and by J. R. Edwards, 'Language attitudes', in E. B. Ryan and H. Giles (eds.), *Attitudes towards Language Variation* (1982). Malcolm Petyt of Reading University reported on a more informal set of evaluations conducted by local radio, in *Locally Speaking*, with Brian Redhead, BBC Radio 4, 9 January 1983. See also Kate Brettell, 'Evaluation of accents among health visitor students', in *Health Visitor*, vol. 60, no. 3, March 1987, and correspondence in May 1987 issue.

p. 59 footnote **Glaswegian accent**: see especially R. K. S. Macaulay and G. Trevelyan, *Language, Social Class, and Education: a Glasgow study* (Edinburgh, 1977), ch. 4 and pp. 4, 28, 112.

p. 60 **Cockneys rate other Cockneys less favourably**: see, for example, Greg Smith (1979) as quoted in R. A. Hudson (1980).

p. 61 **Second-hand car**: reported by Petyt (1983).

p. 61 **Assign occupations**: H. Giles, 'Evaluative reactions to accents', *Educational Review* (Birmingham), no. 22, 1970, 211–27; and Petyt (1983).

p. 61 **Accent in court cases and in doctor-patient and job interviews**: the influence of accent and similar linguistic factors in these contexts has been studied by many researchers, including Rudolf Kalin, 'The social significance of speech in medical, legal and occupational settings', in E. B. Ryan and H. Giles (eds.) (1982); E. A. Lind and W. M. O'Barr, 'The social significance of speech in the courtroom', in H. Giles and R. St Clair (eds.), *Language and Social Psychology* (1979); and in papers by R. Wodak-Engel and Paula Treichler and colleagues in Cheris Kramarae *et al.* (eds.), *Language and Power* (1984).

p. 62 **Educated Scottish Standard English**: see A. J. Aitken in P. Trudgill (ed.), *Language in the British Isles* (1984), 524.

p. 63 **Wyld on merits of RP**: H. C. Wyld, *The Best English*, Society for Pure English (SPE) Tract no. 39 (Oxford, 1934).

p. 63 **Great fan of the Beatles**: quoted in Petyt (1983).

p. 63 **Strong Glaswegian accents**: see R. K. S. Macaulay and G. D Trevelyan (1977) especially ch. 8.

p. 65 **Brainwashing**: one version of this argument can be found in Trudgill (1983), ch. 11, 211 ff.

p. 71 **Majority speak General American**: see Wells (1982), vol. 3, 470–2.

p. 71 **New Yorkers detect non-standard**: Giles and Powesland (1975), 38.

p. 71 **One US observer**: R. Hogan, Preface to NY Board of Education, *Non-standard Dialect* (NCTE, Illinois), quoted in Giles and Powesland (1975), 99.

p. 71 **French-Canadians discriminate:** Giles and Powesland (1975), 49–50.

p. 72 **Birmingham accent experiment:** summarized in Giles and Powesland (1975), 101–4.

p. 74 **Unawareness of own accent:** Andrew Wilkinson, 'Spoken English', in *Educational Review*, Supplement 17 (2) Occasional Publications no. 2, 1965.

p. 74 **Optimum age for foreign language:** see article by James Emil Flege in *Applied Linguistics*, vol. 8, no. 2 (1987). There is a good discussion of age factors in Rod Ellis, *Understanding Second Language Acquisition* (1985), ch. 5.

p. 75 **Accent flexibility declines:** C. F. Hockett, *A Course in Modern Linguistics* (1958).

p. 75 **Educatedness not always encouraged:** note, for example, Bill Naughton, *On a Pig's Back* (1987); comments by Black social worker David Devine on *Profile*, BBC Radio 4, 23 July 1987, about his own upbringing; Anthony Burgess, *Little Wilson and Big God* (1987), 49, 56, 78, 115.

p. 76 **RP enhances women's competence and femininity:** H. Giles and P. Smith, 'Accommodation Theory', in H. Giles and R. St Clair (eds.), *Language and Social Psychology* (1979).

p. 76 **Martha's Vineyard islanders:** described in ch. 2 of William Labov, *Sociolinguistic Patterns* (1972).

p. 77 **RP Welsh language supporters:** observable on *The Fate of the Language* (Welsh), Channel 4 TV, 4 August 1987.

p. 77 **Stronger Welsh accents in English:** see Giles and Powesland (1975), 76; and R. Y. Bourhis and H. Giles, 'The language of intergroup distinctiveness', in H. Giles (ed.), *Ethnicity and Intergroup Relations* (1977).

FIVE: *What is happening to RP?*

p. 82 **"Aggressively northern" Redhead:** *Sunday Times* profile, 3 May 1987.

p. 82 **Percentages considering themselves working class:** item on social trends, *The Times*, 29 January 1987.

p. 83 **Middle-class ambitions of ordinary citizen:** this point has been elaborated in a series of *Sunday Times* articles in 1986–7 by Brian Walden, especially 16 August 1986.

p. 83 **Working class dying:** Jack Straw MP, speaking on *Analysis*, BBC Radio 4, 17 September 1987.

p. 84 **Dustmen's 'fiddles':** extracts in *Sunday Times*, 28 November 1982 from Gerald Mars, *Cheats at Work* (1982).

p. 85 **Street-credibility at Cambridge:** 'Peterborough' in *Daily Telegraph*, 27 July 1987.

p. 85 **Obligatory Oxford Cockney:** Martyn Harris, 'Oxford comes down', *New Society*, 20 June 1986.

p. 86 **Teachers' formal qualifications to teach English:** see John Honey, *The Language Trap* (National Council for Educational Standards, 1983); and *Kingman Report on the Teaching of English Language* (1988).

p. 87 **Teachers downgrade pupils with non-standard accents:** see W. Peter Robinson, 'Speech markers and social class', in H. Giles and K. R. Sherer (eds.) *Social Markers in Speech* (1979), 237, 245; H. Giles and P. Powesland, *Speech Style and Social Evaluation* (1975), 107; Viv Edwards, 'Dialectics', in *Times Educational Supplement*, 2 May 1986; and Ashton Gibson, *The Unequal Struggle* (1986).

p. 87 **Teachers' expectations self-fulfilling:** claims like those of R. Rosenthal and L. Jakobson, *Pygmalion in the Classroom* (1968) of the overwhelming influence of teachers' attitudes on pupil performance are now held to be based on dubious evidence. See especially S. S. Wineburg, 'Self-fulfilling prophecy', in *Educational Researcher*, December 1987 (USA).

p. 87 *Hamlet* **by northern actors:** T. H. Pear, *English Social Differences* (1955), 87.

p. 88 **Decline of actors' English:** comments by Patricia Hayes on *Wogan*, BBC 1, 29 November 1985; Anthony Burgess, in *Observer*, 18 September 1983, 33.

p. 88 **Joe Orton's accent:** John Lahr, *Prick Up Your Ears* (1980), 82, 117.

p. 88 **Leo McKern:** his comments on *Desert Island Discs*, BBC Radio 4, 28 April 1984.

p. 88 **Leonard Rossiter:** obituary in *The Times*, 8 October 1984.

p. 88 **Bill Fraser:** obituary in *The Times*, 7 September 1987.

p. 88 **George Cole and Alistair Sim:** profile of Cole by Peter Lewis, *The Times*, 1 February 1986.

p. 89 **First women BBC TV presenters:** *The Birth of Television*, BBC 2, 30 July 1984.

p. 91 'Popular' London accent: J. C. Wells, *Accents of English* (1982), vol 2, 301–2.

p. 91 Prince Edward: item shown on Independent Television *News*, 16 June 1987.

p. 92 Simon Bates: BBC Radio 1, 6 August 1986.

p. 93 Walter ("Water"): Wells (1982), vol. 2, 314.

p. 94 Galilean *h*-droppers: Geza Vermes, *Jesus the Jew* (1973), 53.

p. 94 Christ's accent in schools programme: *Times Educational Supplement*, 4 October 1985, 32.

p. 95 Single most powerful shibboleth: Wells (1982), vol. I, 254.

p. 95 Stern glance restores dropped *h*: *ibid.*, 254.

p. 95 Bevin's "you and I": Giles and Powesland (1975), 177.

p. 96 A couple of aspirates: one version of this story is given in John Campbell, *F. E. Smith* (1983), 258. This pun was reportedly also used by Anthony Burgess's father in the 1930s: *Little Wilson and Big God* (1987), 48.

SIX: *Accent variety and the mass media*

p. 97 Hours of TV viewing: figures quoted by Geoffrey Sutton in *Daily Mail* article, 5 August 1987.

p. 99 footnote Programme on sexual harassment: BBC Radio 4, 20 August 1982.

p. 100 'Gods' appear as 'guards': letter in *The Times* from Lord Hemingford, 12 October 1982.

p. 100 American 'asses': letter in *Times Higher Education Supplement* from E. Rudd, Department of Sociology, University of Essex, 16 April 1982.

p. 101 I can't understand a word they say: quoted by William Norris in *Times Higher Education Supplement*, 6 September 1985, 8.

p. 101 'Sissy' accents of British spokesmen: T. H. Pear, *English Social Differences* (1955), 96–7.

p. 102 RP preferred accent for theatre classics: *Omnibus*, BBC 1, 7 November 1982.

p. 102 Welsh accent 'unacceptable' for US marketing in Britain: report by Gerald Bartlett in *Daily Telegraph*, 24 April 1986.

p. 102 Pure English spoken in Australia: attributed to J. A. Froude's *Oceania* (1873) by Sidney J. Baker, *The Australian Language* (1945; new edn. 1978), 13.

p. 103 Sydney student changes accent: Donald Horne, *The*

Education of Young Donald (Penguin Australia, 1975), 201. On Australian English see also G. W. Turner, *The English Language in Australia and New Zealand* (2nd edn. 1972).

p. 103 **Hawke's election acknowledgement:** quoted by Fritz Spiegl, *Daily Telegraph*, 18 July 1987.

p. 104 **Advertisement put me off Australia:** letter in *Sunday Times*, 7 December 1986.

p. 104 footnote **To buy or not to buy:** Anthony Holden, *Observer*, 28 April 1981.

p. 105 **India third largest publisher in English:** Anatol Lieven, article in *Times Higher Education Supplement*, 1 June 1984.

p. 105 **Impenetrable Indian accents:** J. C. Wells, *Accents of English* (1982), vol. 3, 624.

p. 106–7 **Different stress pattern of Indian English:** see R. K. Bansal, *The Intelligibility of Indian English* (Hyderabad, 1969) and other works by Bansal and Brian Harrison; Wells (1982), vol. 3, 624–31; and Paroo Nihalani, R. K. Tongue and Priya Hosali, *Indian and British English* (1979). A particularly interesting source is an unpublished PhD thesis, 'Problems of pronunciation of individual words of English as spoken by the teachers of English in the rural schools of the Punjab', by Dr Dharan Vir Jindal, University of the Punjab, Chandigarh, 1985.

p. 107 **Foreign doctors' exam pass rates:** *Daily Telegraph*, 10 May 1986 and item by Stuart Little in *EFL Gazette*, no. 10, 91, July 1987; also a revealing article by Joy Parkinson, 'English language problems of overseas doctors working in the UK', in *ELTJ*, no. 34, 2, January 1980.

p. 108 **Washington judge on Pakistani's accent:** *The Times*, 24 September 1982, 7.

p. 110 **TV documentary on Patagonia:** *Odyssey* series, Channel 4, 15 July 1987.

p. 111 **Listeners' complaints against Welsh, Irish and Michael Parkinson:** *Feedback*, BBC Radio 4, 13 March 1987.

p. 111 **Unintelligibility claim masks prejudice:** Professor Peter Trudgill, 'Talking Proper', *Forty Minutes* series, BBC 2, 17 January 1985.

p. 112 **Susan Rae's comments:** *ibid*.

p. 112 **Item on Crufts:** *Press Review*, BBC Radio 4, 2 February 1986.

p. 113 **Scottish newsreaders' accents:** A. J. Aitken, 'Scots and English in Scotland', in P. Trudgill (ed.), *Language in the British Isles* (1984), 525.

p. 113 **Scottish pupil cites BBC speaker:** item on Ross McMillan and his pupils in 'Talking Proper' (1985).

p. 113 **Isobel Barnett's accent:** information given by a schoolfellow on programme on Lady Barnett, BBC Midlands, 9 November 1982.

p. 113 **Teddy Taylor's "incomprehensible" accent:** Julian Critchley, *Observer*, 10 August 1986.

p. 114 **Scottishness on Radio 4:** John Woodforde, *Daily Telegraph*, 6 January 1985.

p. 115 **Rabble-rouser:** *Daily Mirror*, quoted on *Press Review*, BBC Radio 4, 25 June 1986.

p. 115 **Music-hall joke:** *Sunday Telegraph*, 30 November 1986.

p. 115 **Spirituality of rhinoceros:** Russell Davies, *Observer*, 20 October 1985.

p. 115 **Sinister air, not understanding compatriots:** Paul Ferris, *Observer*, 11 April 1982.

p. 115 **Assertive men, adaptive women, elocution classes:** E. Douglas-Cowie, in P. Trudgill (ed.) (1984), 541, 543.

p. 115 **Journalist poses as corrupt punter:** *Sunday Times*, 14 August 1983.

p. 116 **Friendly, doggy figure:** *The Times*, 30 April 1987.

p. 116 **Bodkin Adams's soft burr:** *Daily Telegraph*, 6 July 1983.

p. 118 **Reaction to Pattie Caldwell:** David Wade, *The Times*, 23 November 1985.

p. 118 **Lorraine Chase:** Paul Ferris, *Observer*, 2 August 1981.

p. 118 **Statuesque starlet:** *Private Eye*, 20 September 1985.

p. 118 **Obsessed with labelling people:** Janet Street-Porter, interviewed on 'Talking Proper' (1985).

p. 119 **Tabloid journalism on air:** Sue Pilkington, *Guardian*, 2 July 1986.

p. 119 **Cockney from Hackney:** 'Mandrake', *Sunday Telegraph*, 5 January 1986.

p. 119 **That extraordinary voice:** Henry Porter, 'Notebook', *Sunday Times*, 23 February 1986.

p. 119 **Reactions to Jameson:** Paul Ferris, *Observer*, 8 June 1986; *Feedback*, BBC Radio 4, 6 June 1986.

p. 119 **Hickory Hollers:** BBC Radio 2, 8 October 1986.

p. 120 **Tumultuous:** BBC Radio 2, 4 August 1986.

p. 120 **Syllables unstressed before:** Porter, 'Notebook', 23 February 1986.

p. 120 **Born ignorant:** *Anything you can do*, BBC 1, 3 May 1987.

p. 120 **Grim reminder of poverty:** Sue Pilkington, *Guardian*, 2 July 1986.

p. 120 **Pretentious waffle:** *Feedback*, BBC Radio 4, 30 June 1986.

p. 121 **We don't say "Tarrah":** review of J. Miller, *Street Talk*, by Robert McCrum, *Sunday Times*, 19 October 1986.

p. 122 **Mother confronts headmaster:** *Brookside*, Channel 4, 11 July 1984.

p. 123 **Taboo programme in some homes:** Michael Smith, *Times Educational Supplement*, 29 May 1987.

p. 123 **Accents on *Grange Hill*:** see especially episode screened on BBC 1, 9 January 1987.

p. 124 **Memorable news presenter:** Anne Karpf, *Guardian*, 22 July 1985.

p. 124 **Newsreaders supplement incomes:** *Sunday Times*, 5 July 1987.

p. 124 **Patricia Hughes's voice and accent:** Anne Chisholm, *Observer*, 6 February 1983.

p. 124 **Bequest to newsreaders:** *The Times*, 19 August 1985, 2.

p. 124 **Journalist in Albania:** *Daily Telegraph*, 19 September 1986.

p. 125 **John Arlott's accent:** Simon Hoggart, *Guardian*, 17 April 1980; personal communication, John Arlott to John Honey, 17 May 1980.

p. 126 **Cheery kinda person:** 'Talking Proper' (1985).

p. 126 **Complaint from Bournville:** letter in *Observer*, 12 April 1981.

p. 127 **Nissan's Sunderland commercial:** David Sapsted, *The Times*, 29 January 1987.

p. 127 **Dr Mitchell on perceptions of accent:** A. Mitchell, 'The real thing', *Sunday Times*, 25 May 1986, extracted from *Britain: a view from Westminster*, ed. Julian Critchley (1986).

p. 128 **John Ardagh:** quoted in Austin Mitchell article, *ibid.*

p. 128 **Glasgow's deprivation but humanity:** review of book on Glasgow, *Sunday Times*, 10 May 1987.

p. 129 **Critic on depressing Birmingham accent:** Paul Ferris, *Observer*, 5 April 1981.

p. 130 **Razor blades on glass:** Susan Raby, *Sunday Times*, 1 June 1986.

p. 130 **BBC radio editor discourages Scouse:** 'PHS', *The Times* diary, 23 September 1986.

SEVEN: *The accents of politics*

p. 132 **Brian Mulroney:** information from Tim Sheppard, Canadian Press Office, London, 21 September 1987.

p. 133 **Walter Mondale:** quoted in *Observer*, 11 November 1984.

p. 134 **Baker as best communicator:** BBC Radio 4, *Today*, 21 May 1986.

p. 134 **Douglas-Home and Brittan:** profile of Brittan by Kent Barker, *World at One*, BBC Radio 4, 15 January 1986.

p. 134 **Mr Gladstone's audiences:** Alan Watkins, 'The shelf-life factor', *Observer*, 15 June 1986.

p. 135 **Align voice with ego:** Jenny Rees, 'How to be the voice of authority', *Daily Telegraph*, 13 April 1987.

p. 136 **Kennedy and Boston aristocracy:** Geoffrey Nunberg, 'The speech of the New York city upper class', in Tim Shopen and J. Williams (eds.), *Standards and Dialects in English* (1980).

p. 136 **Democratic front-runners in 1984:** Washington correspondent Robert Chesshyre, *Observer*, 4 and 5 March 1984.

p. 136 **Unsophisticated Lincolnshire girl:** Nicholas Wapshott and George Brock, *Thatcher* (1983), ch.3.

p. 137 **Divorced from your background:** *ibid*.

p. 137 **Marked RP detectable:** from clip of Margaret Thatcher TV appearance in 1960 shown on *World in Action* programme on freedom of information, ITV, 12 March 1984.

p. 137 **Advice from Gordon Reece:** 'PHS', *The Times* diary item on Reece, 24 March 1983; Pendennis in *Observer*, 12 February 1984.

p. 137 **Enunciation:** Wapshott and Brock (1983), ch.1.

p. 137 **A. J. P. Taylor:** quoted by Piers Brendon, *Observer*, 14 June 1987 from Eva Haraszti Taylor's *A Life with Alan* (1987).

p. 137 **Roedean Water torture:** 'PHS', *The Times* diary, 30 August 1984, citing a hostile biography of Mrs Thatcher by M. McFadyean and M. Ryan (1984).

p. 137 **Schoolmarm:** *Observer*, 15 August 1985.

p. 137 **Southern suburban:** Andrew Neil, *Question Time*, BBC 1, 18 June 1987.

p. 138 **Such a flourish:** Ms Bonney Angelo, US commentator, *Today*, BBC Radio 4, 7 May 1984.

p. 138 **Beryl Bainbridge:** *Observer*, 27 September 1987.

p. 140 **Plum in one's mouth:** *Observer* article on Michael Foot, 20 September 1981.

p. 140 **Bryan Gould at Balliol:** *Times* profile of Gould, 6 November 1986.

p. 140 *Times* **cartoon:** 2 March 1983.

p. 140 footnote **Historic Northumberland r:** Daniel Defoe, *A Tour through the Whole Island of Great Britain* (1724–26), ed. P. Rogers (Penguin ed. 1971), Letter 9, 538.

p. 141 **Disraeli's r-less colleagues:** Disraeli's *Reminiscences*, ed. H. and M. Swartz (1975), 87.

p. 141 **Aneurin Bevan:** see his entry in *Dictionary of National Biography 1951–60.*

p. 141 **Lacked the common touch:** review of the British press, BBC World Service, 14 June 1983.

p. 141 **Castilian nobleman:** Edward Pearce, *Sunday Times*, 16 August 1987.

p. 142 **Mockery of Heath accent:** e.g. *Private Eye*, no. 583, 20 April 1984.

p. 143 **Norman Tebbit:** Peregrine Worsthorne, discussing Tebbit's suitability as a future Tory leader in the *Sunday Telegraph*, 22 December 1985, wrote, "He lacks that desirable touch of class."

p. 143 **Kenneth Clarke's accent:** *Times* profile by Michael Hatfield, 22 May 1986.

p. 144 **Julian Critchley on MPs' accents:** *Observer*, 25 August 1985, and in *Westminster Blues* (1985).

p. 144 **Dear Bill's Tory oiks:** *Private Eye*, no. 600, 14 December 1984.

p. 145 **New-boy MPs:** *Private Eye*, no. 583, 20 April 1984.

p. 145 **Newcastle-under-Lyme by-election:** Alan Watkins, *Observer*, 13 July 1986.

p. 145 **Speech delivery terrible:** *Feedback*, BBC Radio 4, 29 November 1986.

p. 146 **Penhaligon and Common Agricultural Policy:** Margaret Van Hattem, *Financial Times*, 4 January 1986.

p. 146 **Paul Tyler:** *Any Questions?*, BBC Radio 4, 20 January 1984.

p. 146 **Conservatives' foreign accents:** Norman Stone, *Sunday Times*, 14 June 1987.

p. 146 **Marquess of Huntly:** obituary in the *Daily Telegraph*, 28 January 1987.

p. 147 **Giles Radice:** Frank Johnson, *The Times*, 13 July 1983.

p. 147 **Defected from the Labour camp:** report on Christopher, son of Sir F. Catherwood, *Cambridge Evening News*, 27 April 1979.

p. 147 **'Classless' Reptonian MP:** Alan Watkins, *Observer*, 6 April 1986.

p. 147 **Skinner's accent:** *Financial Times*, 4 January 1986.

p. 148 **Larry Whitty:** *Observer* profile, 3 February 1985.

p. 148 **Rude and menacing accents:** Alan Watkins, *Observer*, 7 October 1984 (my italics).

p. 149 **Off-duty market trader:** *Observer* profile of Todd, 16 June 1985.

p. 149 **Norman Willis's TUC address:** extract on Channel 4 News, 5 September 1985.

p. 150 **Darlington by-election candidate:** Alan Watkins, *Observer*, 20 March 1983.

EIGHT: *Changing patterns*

p. 152 **Restaurant manager:** *The Times*, 4 April 1984.

p. 152 **Sales executive:** *Daily Telegraph*, 24 July 1985.

p. 152 **Administrative assistant:** *The Times*, 17 August 1987.

p. 152 **The General Manager:** *The Times*, 1 October 1983.

p. 152 **Film role for seventeen-year-old:** *The Times*, 3 April 1985.

p. 153 **Accents cause unemployment:** Liz Hodgkinson, *The Times*, 3 September 1985 and letters, 11 September 1985.

p. 153 **A. L. Rowse:** see especially his *A Man of the Thirties* (1979) and *A Cornish Childhood* (1942).

p. 153 **Accents in Taylor family:** A. J. P. Taylor, *A Personal History* (1983), ch. 1, and pp. 80, 86.

p. 154 **Accents in Burgess's family:** Anthony Burgess, *Little Wilson and Big God* (1987), 11–12, 87, 243 and ff.

p. 154 **Alan Bullock and chancellorship:** Graham Turner, *Sunday Telegraph* feature, 8 February 1987.

p. 154 **Norman Chester obituary:** *The Times*, 22 September 1986.

p. 156 **Young women of gentle birth**: Alan Watkins, *Observer*, 29 September 1985.

p. 156 **Obligatory in caring professions**: Peter Ackroyd, *The Times*, 7 January 1984.

p. 157 **Teachers adopt slovenly speech**: Diana Bramwell, quoted by John Izbicki in *Daily Telegraph*, 9 May 1983.

p. 157 **Paul Foot's accent nightmare**: *Any Questions?*, BBC Radio 4, 27 April 1984.

p. 157 **Peter Bowles's accent**: Bowles, interviewed on 'Talking Proper', BBC 2, 17 January 1985.

p. 158 **Michael Caine on accent**: Stephen Fry, 'Laid back and thinking of England', *Sunday Times* colour supplement, 12 May 1985.

p. 158 **ITV documentary on fourteen children**: *28–up*, Central TV, 19, 20 and 21 November 1984.

p. 159 **Healey's code-switching**: Simon Hoggart, *Observer*, 22 May 1983.

p. 160 **Press comment on Tatchell**: see, for example, letters in *Daily Telegraph*, 24 February 1983; and Ivan Rowan, *Sunday Telegraph*, 27 February 1983.

p. 160 **J. B. Priestley on dishonest accent changers**: I have been unable to tract the exact location of these comments, quoted very precisely to me by my colleagues, and would welcome information on this and other observations by Priestley on accent. His description of the Tyneside accent is in Chapter 9 of *English Journey* (1934).

p. 161 **Black Pentecostalist pastor**: BBC 1, 19 August 1984.

p. 161 **Afro adaptation of Barbara**: *Sunday Times*, 17 April 1983.

p. 161 **US evaluation of Black voices**: H. Giles and P. Powesland, *Speech Style and Social Evaluation* (1975), 81.

p. 162 **Black Cardiff children**: *ibid.*, 43.

p. 162 **Diane Abbott profile**: see 1987 *Observer* article 'The naughty girl who made good', by Christian Wolmar.

p. 163 **Blacks beginning to break through**: Bernie Grant MP, interviewed in *Profile* by Sally Hardcastle, BBC Radio 4, 25 June 1987.

p. 164 **Well-spoken Mugabe**: Alec Smith, *Now I Call Him Brother* (1984), 119 (my italics).

p. 164 **London Jewish accent**: J. C. Wells, *Accents of English* (1982), vol. 2, 303.

p. 164 **London homosexual accent**: *ibid.*, vol. 1, 21–2.

NINE: *Accents and the future*

p. 167 **An explosion of English**: for a discussion of estimates of present totals of mother-tongue and second-language speakers of English throughout the world see David Crystal, 'How many millions? The statistics of English today' in *English Today*, Issue no. 1, January 1985.

p. 167 **British English as international standard**: Rudolph C. Bambas, *The English Language: its origin and history* (Oklahoma, 1980), 218.

p. 170 **Teach foreigners regional accents**: see especially R. Atkinson, 'RP and English as a world language' in *International Review of Applied Linguistics*, no. 23, 69–72; also Leo Loveday, *The Sociolinguistics of Learning and Using a Non-Native Language* (1982), chs. 5 and 6.

p. 170 **German girl of eighteen**: *The Times*, 18 June 1983.

p. 170 **Japanese school of English**: *Times Educational Supplement*, 6 September 1985.

p. 175 **Child's right to an open future**: the phrase comes from J. Feinberg, 'The child's right to an open future', in W. Aiken and D. H. Lafollette (eds.), *Whose Child? Children's rights, parental authority and state power* (1980), 124–53. I owe this reference to Roger Marples of Southlands College, Wimbledon.

p. 175 **Good fairy's gift**: *News Chronicle*, June 1956, cited by T. H. Pear in *Personality, Appearance and Situation* (1957), 77.

p. 175 **Jim Davidson's ambitions for son**: *Wogan*, BBC 1, 9 April 1983.

p. 177 **Christine Keeler's speech**: *Observer*, 13 March 1983.

p. 180 **Post-Second World War politician**: This remark was attributed to Sir Harold Nicolson by a *Guardian* writer around 1978, but I have been unable to trace its exact source, nor can his son, Nigel Nicolson, provide the precise reference. I should be grateful for help on this.

p. 181 **"No bleedin' fear!"**: this point has been made by the expert on Cockney, Julian Franklyn.

p. 181 **School-leaver's job opportunities**: for examples of employers' comments on non-standard accents, see R. K. S. Macaulay and G. D. Trevelyan, *Language, Social Class and Education: a Glasgow study* (Edinburgh, 1977), ch. 8.

Index